MARCO ⊕ POLO

T0166881

DUB ROV NIK

AND DALMATIAN COAST

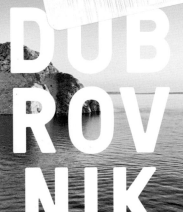

AUSTRIA
Villach
HUNGARY
SLOVENIA
Ljubljana   Zagreb
ITALY
Trieste
CROATIA
Rijeka
SERBIA
CROATIAN
COAST/
DALMATIA
BOSNIA
HERZEGOVINA
Sarajevo
Ancona
Split
MONTE-
NEGRO
*Adriatic
Sea*
Dubrovnik

www.marco-polo.com

FREE!

THE
TOURING APP
shows you the way ...
including routes and offline maps!

GET MORE OUT OF YOUR MARCO POLO GUIDE

IT'S AS SIMPLE AS THIS

1 go.marco-polo.com/ddc

2 download and discover

GO!

WORKS OFFLINE!

SYMBOLS

 INSIDER TIP — Insider Tip

★ Highlight

🟢🟢🟢⚫ Best of...

 Scenic view

 Responsible travel: for eco-
logical or fair trade aspects

(*) Telephone numbers
that are not toll-free

**PRICE CATEGORIES
HOTELS**

Expensive	over 1,150 kuna
Moderate	600–1,150 kuna
Budget	under 600 kuna

Prices are for two people in a
double room per night, including breakfast, in peak
season

**PRICE CATEGORIES
RESTAURANTS**

Expensive	over 230 kuna
Moderate	150–230 kuna
Budget	under 150 kuna

Prices for a typical meal on
the restaurant's menu con-
sisting of starter, main course,
dessert and one drink

CONTENTS

KARTEN IM BAND
(138 A1) Page numbers and coordinates refer to the road atlas
(0) Site/address located off the map

Coordinates are also given for places that are not marked on the road atlas

(𝌆 A–B 2–3) refers to the removable pull-out map

INSIDE FRONT COVER:
The best Highlights

INSIDE BACK COVER:
Maps of Dubrovnik, Split, Trogir and Zadar

The best MARCO POLO Insider Tips

Our top 15 Insider Tips

INSIDER TIP Twisting pasta
If you're not put off by the idea of cooking on holiday, try your hand at making *Žrnovski makaruni* pasta in the traditional way by turning dough on sticks at *Konoba Belin* on the island of Korčula which you are invited to taste afterwards → **p. 92**

INSIDER TIP Clifftop panorama
The view from the top of *Kliff Grpašćak* is simply spectacular, with the southwest coast of Dugi otok rising impressively from the sea in a huge wall of rock → **p. 38**

INSIDER TIP Swim among ancient ruins
Ugljan's idyllic *Vela Luka* beach is surrounded by Roman archaeological sites, which are unfortunately not signposted – but it's fun to hunt them down! → **p. 44**

INSIDER TIP Life with a Latin twist
The rainbow colours and relaxed atmosphere of *Abuela's Beach House* in Brela lend a Caribbean touch to the Makarska Riviera → **p. 63**

INSIDER TIP Dancing in the water tank
Located in a former cistern beneath Šibenik's fountain square, the *Azimut* club is the meeting point for the town's alternative scene. Its high vault ceiling and authentic retro-style furniture create the perfect vibe for live concerts → **p. 40**

INSIDER TIP Seaside games
Split's city beach *Bačvice* is a meeting point for *picigin* players – get involved! → **p. 68**

INSIDER TIP Go kayaking among God's tears
Grab your paddle and let *Malik Adventures* show you the most beautiful islands in the fascinating Kornati archipelago – and if you want to, you can do yoga afterwards! → **p. 35**

INSIDER TIP California in Croatia
Try your hand at *mandarin picking* (photo above) on the Neretva delta, aka The Green Valley → **p. 87**

INSIDER TIP Salty souvenirs

The lagoons around Nin have a long tradition of salt production, and the salt works *museum shop* sells delicious salty specialties –try the salty chocolate → **p. 50**

INSIDER TIP Ride a sea kayak into the sunset

Take to the water with *Hvar Adventure* on a guided paddle tour of Hvar's old town for an unusual perspective on this jet-set hot spot → **p. 57**

INSIDER TIP Pitch your tent on a terrace

Camp Grebišće in Jelsa on the island of Hvar is located on a deep and exceptionally idyllic cove, with a wonderful beach of fine shingle → **p. 60**

INSIDER TIP Paradise cove

It admittedly takes a lot of effort to make it down (and then back up again) into this secluded bay on the island of Vis – but the shingle cove of *Uvala Stiniva,* with its bright turquoise waters almost completely encircled by high cliffs, is absolutely stunning → **p. 105**

INSIDER TIP Secret gem in the Old Town

Chic B&B in Stari Grad with very hospitable owners. Stray cats are also offered an abode in the *Hidden House* → **p. 60**

INSIDER TIP Hawk's eye view

From the *Sokol grad* fort, which literally translates as falcon city due to many falconers who once lived there, you have amazing bird's eye views along the entire Konavle valley → **p. 78**

INSIDER TIP A capon in Dubrovnik

The restaurant *Kopun* doesn't just enjoy a thoroughly romantic location – it also serves specialities from other parts of Croatia, such as capon → **p. 84**

BEST OF...

GREAT PLACES FOR FREE
Discover new places and save money

FOR FREE

● *Art in white stone*
Visit the *Galerija Jakšić* in Donji Humac on Brač to see how generations of Croatian artists have worked and continue to work with the island's precious marble; viewings are free of charge → p. 56

● *Monastic treasures in a beautiful location*
Most monasteries on the Croatian coast charge admission fees. The Benedictines of *Sv. Kuzma i Damjan* near Tkon are still not charging an entrance fee to show off their beautifully situated abbey and Gothic church, whose portal bears Glagolitic inscriptions → p. 44

● *Underwater museum*
There is no admission fee to view the sarcophagus submerged off the coast of Silba, which dates from late antiquity – all you need to visit this *underwater museum* is a diving mask and snorkel → p. 51

● *A promontory of ancient buildings*
There is currently no admission fee to visit the foundations of a Roman bath and the cemetery of a *Greek necropolis* located on the peninsula by the town of Vis, on the island of the same name → p. 73

● *Medieval picture book*
You could spend several hours gazing at the portal of *Trogir Cathedral* without running out of new discoveries. The Old and New Testaments were chiselled into the stone, as if in a frenzy. They can be seen perfectly well from the square without paying a cent (photo) → p. 71

● *Well-maintained lido with a view of Zadar*
The municipal authorities of Preko on the island of Ugljan take the comfort of their guests very seriously, and when renovating their *public lido* they even thought of adding showers, sun loungers and access ladders down to the sea – all of it free of charge. Not many public baths are that comfortable! → p. 43

● *No boundary between land and sea*
The fact that the Dalmatian island world consists of peaks whose mountains were submerged is nowhere so palpable as on the island of Dugi otok, especially if you take to the *panoramic road* with your mountain bike → **p. 37**

● *A beach with a monastery*
The shingle beach of *Martinšćica,* near Bol, lies just behind Brač's famous Golden Cape, on a gently curving bay with crystal-clear waters and an idyllic monastery located on the peninsula. A typical Dalmatian scene → **p. 54**

● *Get out onto the water*
Make sure you see the *old town of Korčula* from the water too. From this perspective, its typically Dalmatian ensemble of buildings – with a cathedral, an episcopal palace and their surrounding rows of houses – really comes into its own → **p. 90**

● *Sweet sounds*
When the people of Dalmatia sing, then they usually do so a cappella and with many parts. In July, the best *klapa choirs* go head to head in the town of Omiš → **p. 122**

● *A district with an authentic ambience*
The *Varoš* quarter of Zadar's old town has avoided the tourists and souvenir shops that fill the rest of the city. This district of bakeries, hairdressers, original boutiques and neighbourhood cafés transforms into a nightlife hot spot after dark (photo) → **p. 47**

● *Island hopping*
Everything that the people living on the Elaphiti Islands need is brought in by ferry – from letters and parcels to chickens and washing machines. Climb aboard too to gain an *insight into everyday island life in Dalmatia* – including a rest stop on the sandy beach of Lopud → **p. 121**

● *Breathtaking panorama*
The reward for the steep climb from Hvar's *Pjaca* up to the *Španjola Fortress* is a typically Dalmatian panorama: at ur feet, the houses of the old town, the harbour speckled with boats, beyond them the green dots of the *Pakleni otoci* floating in the blue of the Adriatic → **p. 58**

ONLY IN

BEST OF...

● *Shopping in the emperor's palace*

Diocletian's Palace in Split's old town, the most important building from Roman times in Dalmatia, is well worth a visit. Nice for browsing: the jewellery and souvenir stalls under the vaults, the *podrumi* (photo) → p. 68

● *Thrilling fortifications*

The magnificent *Sv. Ivan Fortress* in Dubrovnik contains not one but two exhibitions: a fascinating aquarium, and a maritime museum explaining all there is to know about naval transport → p. 80

● *A shopping paradise for fashionistas*

Fashion-forward holidaymakers can get their money's worth on rainy days in Zadar's *Supernova Centar.* This shopping centre contains a wide selection of shops, cafés and food outlets to keep visitors busy → p. 48

● *The first base jumper*

The first man to jump with a parachute from a tower was the Šibenik inventor Faust Vrančić. Models and plans from this innovative genius are on display at the *Memorijalni centar* in Prvić → p. 43

● *A visit to the master*

When it rains, one of the suburbs of Split is a good destination. Here Croatia's most famous sculptor, *Ivan Mestrović,* set up his studio. His works, which are monumental, disturbing and fascinating, will bring exciting insights into 20th century art → p. 67

● *A shipwreck with its cargo*

Hundreds of years underwater have not damaged the contents of the Venetian galleon on display in the *City Museum* of Biograd na Moru – the goods are preserved in the same condition as when the ship sank back in the 16th century → p. 33

RAIN

RELAX AND CHILL OUT
Take it easy and spoil yourself

● *The home of peace and quiet*
The name of the famous saltwater lake in *Telašćica Nature Park* says it all: "Mir", meaning "peace". Here, amid small islands, quiet coves and hillsides sprinkled with macchia, it feels as though the world is holding its breath → **p. 38**

● *Paradise on earth*
Biblijski vrt, the "biblical garden" in Stomorija near Kaštel Novi, is a heavenly retreat from earthly stress where you can relax daggling your feet from the stone bridge over the romantic stream or picnicking on the grass → **p. 69**

● *The beauty of oranges*
The gates of Dubrovnik are sometimes closed when there are too many tourists in the city. When that happens, escape to the cloister of the *Dominican monastery* and meditate in the shade of fragrant orange trees → **p. 79**

● *Hvar's quieter side*
While luxury yachts jostle for moorings and VIPs compete for attention in Hvar, at the Pension *Tonči* on the neighbouring island of Sveti Klement the only sounds are the chirp of cicadas and the soothing murmur of the waves → **p. 59**

● *The song of the waves*
The *sea organ* must be one of the loveliest spots in Zadar – sit on the steps of this acoustic artwork and listen to the melodies the sea brings to life in it (photo) → **p. 45**

● *Taking time out*
Being alone with just a few skippers and the people who live on *Lopud*. The Elaphiti Island possesses one thing aplenty: peace and quiet. Rent a room in one of the elegant, small family hotels and wait until the day-trippers have left the island. Then you will have the island all to yourself → **p. 89**

INTRODUCTION

DISCOVER THE CROATIAN COAST!

Imagine the following: 1,777 km (1,100 miles) of coastline, off which there are a total of 1,184 islands. Most of the islands lie directly off the Dalmatian coast in the Adriatic. There are large ones such as Brač and tiny ones such as Lokrum, *inhabited islands and inhospitable rocky reefs*, lavishly green ones and ones only suitable for sheep grazing. Some are given a jagged appearance by their countless bays, while others are lined by beaches. An absolute dream destination! It is not surprising that this coastline is one of Europe's *most beautiful sailing spots* and a holiday landscape whose diverse appeals, changing moods, ruggedness and charm will create lasting memories.

Locals are proud to claim they inhabit the most beautiful place on the planet and with its translucent blue sea, historically-rooted buildings and magnificent olive oil you can kind of understand why. Yet visit Split's palace district or Dubrovnik's old town walls, follow the sweet smell of ripe oranges, watch the *swarms of fish swimming through your feet* in the crystal-clear waters, spend an evening drinking your cares away with a glass of wine in a traditional konoba and be blown away by the almost kitschy beauty of the picturesque coast-

Photo: The beach by the Dominican monastery near Bol, on the island of Brač

A popular promenade by day and night: Luža Square and the Sponza Palace in Dubrovnik

line from the ferry – and you too are bound to fall in love with this spectacular spot on earth.

The peaks of the Dinaric Alps, which reach an altitude of 1,700 m (5,577 ft), create a dramatic barrier to inland Croatia.

> **The people's lives are oriented towards the sea**

Squeezed between the range and the sea are coastal towns, while *grapes, oranges, olives and palm trees* flourish, sheltered from the wind by the mountains. This unusual landscape is still quite young. The coastal range was only flooded after the most recent ice age; the peaks were transformed into islands, the valleys into straits. When travelling by coastal ferry, this process of formation is particularly visible on the trip through the archipelago of Zadar: the islands of Ugljan and Dugi otok lie on either side, and in between is the small island of Iž.

1st millennium BC – 2nd century AD
The Illyrians, Greeks and finally the Romans settle in Dalmatia and found trading posts

6th–10th centuries
Dalmatia is Byzantine; Slavs immigrate into the area; founding of the first Croatian kingdom

from the 12th century onwards
Dalmatia subject to Venice. From the mid-15th century Ottoman troops threaten the coast

1797–1918
Venetian rule comes to an end under Napoleon. The same thing happens to Ragusa in 1808. Austria takes over the legacy of these trading powers

About the ferries in general: even if you stay on the mainland, take at least one day trip by regular ferry to the offshore islands, as there is no nicer way to get to know this coastline, where the boundary between water and land seems to disappear. On a boat trip it also becomes very evident how all the people here live facing the sea. The many little ports, *characterized by Venetian influences*, present their most beautiful side to the water. The wide open expanse, faraway places and the longing to depart to different

> **Deep gorges and gurgling rivers**

shores are constantly present here. This sentiment is reflected most beautifully in *Dalmatian music*, the traditional songs of the *klapa* choirs. The sentiment can also be felt in the pop-music versions by Tomislav Bralić, probably the most popular interpreter of modern Dalmatian music. Sadly, his versions often turn out to be pure schmaltz.

Many legends are told about the formation of the Dalmatian coast, of God's wonderful creation in this otherwise incredibly harsh landscape. Did He really cry on the bare rocks, whereupon His tears turned into islands? Or did He randomly throw a handful of white pebbles onto the coast which just happened to fall into such a beautiful formation? In any case, He was also generous to the land behind the mountain ridge: there are *deep gorges* with rivers winding their way through them, such as in Paklenica National Park and Cetina Gorge, in Krka National Park, where the Krka River gurgles over limestone steps, and in the enchanting landscape of Plitvice Lakes National Park, which is also a Unesco

from 1918
Croats, Serbs and Slovenes found the kingdom of Yugoslavia, which surrenders in World War II (1941)

1939–45
Partisan groups fight against the German Wehrmacht

1945
Founding of the "Federal Republic of Yugoslavia" under Prime Minister Josip Broz Tito

1980
After Tito's death the multi-ethnic state sees the growth of nationalism and an economic crisis

1991
Croatia declares its independence, attack by the Yugoslav army

World Heritage Site. If you like hiking and climbing, getting out into the hills on a mountain bike or going kayaking, then this nature reserve and the others will be just the thing.

In the past the Dalmatians were *great seafarers*. They sailed all the way to America in their boats. These days they are still equipping oil platforms with small, agile lifeboats. In the shipyards they convert fishing boats into leisure craft. The great era of shipbuilding is long over, however. Although the economy is growing, the financial difficulties of the region's two major corporate organizations Agrokor and INA are taking their toll on the national treasury. Unemployment is high, particularly among young people. Young Croats are looking for jobs in other EU countries. Tourism on the coast, however, is booming, which makes Dalmatia one of the richest regions in the country.

Dalmatia's history has been eventful right from the start. In the colonnaded court-yard in Diocletian's Palace in Split, you are intimately surrounded by nearly two thousand years of history. By the columns and arches of a Roman palace. By a pre-Romanesque stone relief in the baptistery, evidence of an era during which Croatia was an independent kingdom and during which it opened up to Christianity. By Gothic carvings on church doors, which were made when Venice subjugated almost the whole of Dalmatia. By the Baroque frenzy of the cathedral's interior, which celebrates *Dalmatia's golden age*. The modern era is also represented here. The people of Split like to while away an hour in the pleasant Café Luxor on the peristyle, enjoying an espresso and reading the paper.

> **2,000 years of history in a small space**

Only the ancient Greeks failed to immortalize themselves here, but they left their mark elsewhere. On the sea floor, for example, where hundreds of amphorae from *sunken merchant vessels* provide special motifs for divers in addition to the already biodiverse underwater world. The ancient Greeks also left their mark on the island of Hvar, or, to be precise, on Stari Grad Plain, where the farmers have, for the past 2,000 years, continuously used the boundaries set by the Greek colonists in around 400 BC.

1995
Croats, Serbs and Bosnians sign a peace treaty

2013
Joins the EU

2015
The International Court of Justice dismisses the genocide claims against Serbia and Croatia. Kolinda Grabar-Kitarović is the first woman to be elected President of Croatia

2017
The UN International Criminal Tribunal sentences six Bosnian-Croat officials for their crimes against the Muslim population

Travertine, cascades and basins: The Krka River meanders spectacularly through the karst landscape

Stari Grad Plain is a Unesco World Heritage Site, as is Diocletian's Palace in Split, the wonderful Šibenik Cathedral, the romantic old town of Trogir and the old town of Dubrovnik. The latest sites on the Dalmatian Coast to be added to this list are the St. Nicholas Fortress on the island of Ljuljevac and Zadar's episcopal complex. As the Republic of Ragusa, the city managed to withstand the Venetians and the Turks alike, usually through cunning and skilled negotiation. Today Dubrovnik has to withstand the crowds of people that flood in through its old city wall every summer from aeroplanes and cruise ships, because the city is one of the *top destinations in Europe* and a must for all globetrotters. The city and its people put up with this patiently and elegantly, like the inhabitants of Hvar, the town that is popularly compared to Marbella and Ibiza. The romantic little town on the island of lavender is up at the top of the to-do list of celebs and starlets.

> **Crowds of people in Dubrovnik's old town**

Go on a journey of discovery! Let yourself wander aimlessly along - be prepared to go off the beaten track and don't worry if you get lost down the side streets: In the worst case, you will end up at one of the many *secluded bays, konobas or small bars*. Hospitality is written big in Dalmatia. Join locals in a glass of rakija, the popular tipple in the Balkans – you only have to take a few sips to be sociable! Even when sober, you'll see Dalmatia through rose-coloured spectacles: The tranquil and often harsh beauty of the islands and bays, the crystal-clear water, the romantic backdrop of medieval ports, fancy restaurants behind rustic walls and finally a beach lounge lit by flares: all these things await.

WHAT'S HOT

1 Original gifts to take back home

Souvenirs Resist the temptation to buy a cheesy dolphin figurine at the souvenir stall – young artists show what locals believe is typically Dalmatian. T-shirts by *Đeloza Dizajn (www.facebook.com/delozadizajn)* in Split combine Dalmatian words of wisdom with creative drawings. The designer label's slogan is "Uvik kontra" (always against) and uses fish to symbolize the defiant attitude associated with Dalmatian people – one fish swimming against the tide. Locals also wear with pride the colourful prints of *Omiš Originals (www.facebook.com/OMIS-Originals-1629155153966195)*; a particular favourite is the "local vocal", a Minecraft figure modelled on a traditional Dalmatian klapa singer. Artist *Luka Mimica (www.facebook.com/blootal)* from Split incorporates high-quality craftsmanship into his models of Croatian islands made from sand taken directly from the beach and blue synthetic resin.

2

Insta-fashion

3

Fashion bloggers from Dalmatia Times have changed since major designers were the only movers and shakers of the fashion industry. Young fashion bloggers are seriously influential. With a bit of style, camera and lots of mascara, they post pics of themselves online in their favourite outfits. Based in the old town of Zadar, the beauty blogger *Sandra Župan Miyagi (@sandramiyagi)* has a whole host of followers on Instagram, all interested in her make-up tutorials. *Lucija Kontić (www.shippedfromvenus.com)* was born in Šibenik, now lives in Split and showcases her romantic and cute fashion ideas in feminine look. Now famous in Croatia, *Sonja Dvornik* takes photos of way-out fashion styles paraded on the streets of Split *(@sonjadvornik | facebook.com/klikom-svud-Sonja-Dvornik)*.

Sun, sea and beats

Summer festivals   Music fans come flocking to the coast every year for its wide variety of festivals which are lined up back to back in the music calendar. Besides traditional *klapa* and classical music, there is something on offer to suit every taste, however alternative. Split vibrates every year to the beats of electronic music at *Ultra Europe (photo)* while Tisno on Murter and Šibenik also belong to the most popular venues for electro/techno sounds hosting the events *Defected* and *Love International.* Local rock and alternative artists play at *Regius* and the *OFF Jazz & Blues Festival* is a must for jazz aficionados. Some of the islands also host festivals such as the street art and hip-hop festival *Graffiti na gradele* in Bol on the island of Brač. More information available at *www.croatiamusicfestivals.com*

Back to idyllic roots

In the Dalmatian hinterland   Everything was better in the old days! Is this longing for a simple, rural way of life the reason why open-air museums are popping up everywhere? The traditional Croatian way of living is creatively brought to life in ethno villages with restored old stone houses, hearty food in authentic konobas and all kinds of attractions. The largest of these is Škopljanci *(Radošić | tel.021 80 57 77 | www.radosic. com)* which even organises a village Olympics and bullfights *(bikijada).* This nostalgic idyllic setting is not only a popular venue for weddings, music videos are also filmed here, for example those of the Croatian singers Severina and Branko Medak. The Split-based fashion designer Monika Sablić also used an ethno village as a shooting location for her latest collection.

19

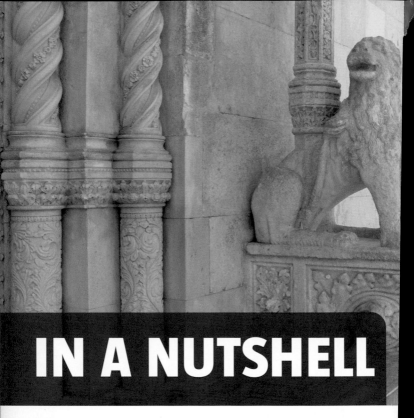

IN A NUTSHELL

TREASURE ISLANDS

What's it like living in the "country of a thousand islands?" you may ask? Some say a thousand while others claim many more – the actual number of islands varies considerably depending on whether you painstakingly count every single rocky outcrop. The coastline is dotted with islands in literally every size and shape (there is even a heart-shaped one amongst them, Galešnjak). They all have one thing in common though: each island is a world of its own. Many city dwellers dream away boring office hours imagining life on a desert island. However, unreliable connections to the mainland, a shortage of water and a lack of community can make life on these islands anything but paradise. When the hefty Bora wind blows its heavy gusts and stops the ferry service for days on end, many islanders are totally cut off from work and medical care, making it a solitary existence. If island life still appeals to you, you can try cutting yourself off from civilisation by spending a holiday in a lighthouse (for example *Veli rat* (see p. 37) on the island Dugi otok).

DALMATIANS AND HOW THEY TICK

Could you accuse the Dalmatians of being lazy? Well it's true they are known for their casual and relaxed way of living. Life here definitely takes a slower pace and the word stress does not seem to be in their vocabulary. It's not a coincidence that a popular Dalmatian saying

Architects, choirs and Robinson feelings, as well as facts about inventions and fan passions of all kinds

goes, "Man is born tired and lives to rest". But don't believe any stereotype that claims Dalmatians do not lift a finger – the only time of day when this applies is during the midday heat when only the naïve tourist can be spotted wandering the streets. The fact is Dalmatians work on average more than the supposedly arrogant *purgeri* (a term which stems from the word "citizen", meaning people who live in the country's capital Zagreb). In Croatia, those living by the coast regard their city-dwelling counterparts with suspicion. How can you seriously want to live somewhere without the fresh sea breeze in your nostrils, they cry and refuse to believe there is anywhere nicer on the planet than the Adriatic. They see their villages through rose-coloured spectacles and only a fool will try and convince a Dalmatian that there are indeed more beautiful beaches elsewhere in the world. If you do, you'll witness their *dišpet,* a stubborn streak which Dalmatians carry around with pride. Above all though, the characteristics you'll en-

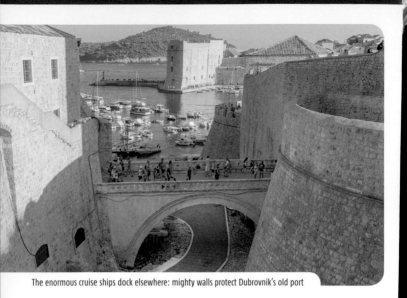

The enormous cruise ships dock elsewhere: mighty walls protect Dubrovnik's old port

counter the most on your travels will be their hospitality, friendliness and their infinite energy to turn every occasion into a celebration, never mind how small.

TYING A KNOT IN MENS' FASHION

If France lays claims to being the mother of fashion, then Croatia is definitely the grandmother, or let's say the great step-aunt at least. The reason is that the tie, or cravat, originally comes from Croatia. According to legend, in 1663, while the Palace of Versailles was under construction, King Louis XIV of France ordered a parade of troops in front of the building site. Marching alongside the regiments were Croatian mercenaries, whose chests were decorated with cloth rosettes attached to their collars. Louis was impressed with this accessory, decreed that his nobles should wear it too, and thus the *cravate* (derived from the French word *croate)* set out on its journey towards global popularity. Although it's

true that the word "cravate" is derived from "Croat", the rest of the story is almost certainly a fiction.

GONE WITH THE WIND

In a country of sailors and islands, wind is not just a matter for small talk. Wind and its strength are an integral part of life for Croatians. The mighty *Bora* wind makes its presence felt especially in autumn and winter when it is capable of bringing the entire infrastructure to a standstill: ferry services stop, streets are blocked and old towns all along the coast are flooded. It blows in from the north east reaching speeds of up to 200 km/h (just for comparison's sake: gale-force strengths are from speeds of 118 km/h). One thing is sure: Never go out to sea when the Bora is in town. The wind's ferocity is not only capable of casting ships far out to sea, it has even been known to catapult coaches into the water. Other winds include the *Maestral* and the *Jugo* or *Scirocco*, less known perhaps but

A long piece of ... started life in Croatia

equally as treacherous, the northwesterly Maestral is said to bring fair weather with high waves and a lot of spray. On the other hand, the Sirocco from the South is not only supposed to blow in sand from the Sahara but also a depressive mood across the land. In the city-state of Dubrovnik, the wind was once a mitigating factor in the courtroom. Offenders were said to receive a milder punishment if the Jugo was blowing at the time they committed their crime. More dangerous than the strong winds put together is the feared draught. What sounds peculiar is in fact taken deadly seriously in the entire southern Slavic region and every child is warned of its perils. Illnesses, diseases, mood swings, family problems can all be attributed to the fact that two windows were left open and a draught was blowing. .

LIVE, BREATHE, EAT FOOTBALL

You may be driving towards Split and suddenly notice the name written on every corner, graffiti-sprayed on every third wall, on the sign above the local baker or printed large on beach towels. Hajduk Split is Croatia's oldest football club, founded in 1911 and worshipped by the locals. The archenemy of every genuine Hajduk fan is Dinamo Zagreb and the legendary rivalry between the two clubs has been known to break out in violence over the years. For this reason, never walk around Dalmatia sporting Dinamo souvenirs unless you're looking for trouble. Hajduk fans, especially the infamous hooligans belonging to the ultra-fan club base Torcida, are reportedly linked to far-right ideologies and are seen wearing T-shirts with the German phrase "Hajduk Jugend" (Hajduk Youth) which has obvious connotations with the Hitler Youth. This fanatical love-hate relationship over

football has its limits though, est fires raged over Split in the of 2011, fans of Hajduk Split and remained side by side to fight the

HIGHLY SKILLED TRIO

Italian Renaissance artists such as Michelangelo are widely known, but few people have probably heard of the names Juraj Dalmatinac, Nikola Firentinac or Andrija Aleši? Right? (We won't tell anyone if you promise to remember their names from now on!). Yet these architects and sculptors are in fact the ambassadors of the Dalmatian Renaissance. In Venetian times, Dalmatia was dominated by Gothic architecture and if the conservative councillors had had it their way in the 14th and 15th century, it would have stayed this way. They rejected point blank the ideas of the rebellious youth and the new emerging style – that was until this trio set the Renaissance movement rolling in Dalmatia with their Italian, humanistic influences. The Dalmatian trademark is an eclectic mixture of old and new, Gothic and other styles influenced by the Renaissance. As his Italian name Giorgio da Sebenico (1410–1475) indicates, he came from Šibenik; however he began his career in Venice where he worked on the Scuola di San Marco, among other projects. In Dalmatia he designed multiple palaces and the cathedral altar in Split, the cathedral in Šibenik (in front of which stands his monument), and the fortifications of Dubrovnik. His colleague, the Tuscan Nikola Firentinac (Niccolò di Giovanni Fiorentino, 1418–1506), imported the style of his homeland to Dalmatia and collaborated with Dalmatinac on Šibenik Cathedral. He may have introduced Dalmatinac to Renaissance ideas in the first place. A frequent third collaborator on significant projects was Andri-

...ndrea Alessi, 1425–1505), a ...usly talented sculptor from Al-... whose best-known works include ...side chapel in Trogir Cathedral – a ...nt effort with Firentinac. The works of these three masters dominate the architectural landscape of towns in Dalmatia even today.

VIRUS-FREE ZONE

It's a well-known fact that the spotted 101 dogs from the famous Disney film got their name from Dalmatia, did you know that the word qua... was also coined here at a time wh... matia as it stands today did not ye... ist and the autonomous city-state of D... brovnik (then known as Ragusa) was one of the most important trading and shipping posts in the South. As such, its citizens were exposed to all types of viruses and diseases from around the world. In the battle against the Plague in the 14th century, the first quarantine camps were set up in Dubrovnik to contain the rapid spread of the Black Death. The word "quarantine" comes from the Italian word

quaranta for "quaranta giorni", meani... forty days, the period that all ships... required to be isolated in cam... which was known as *lazare*... sengers and crew coul... lazareti building in ... today, not as a ... venue for lo...

ce... poin... of July... *kralj*, last ... are sailed in... king then bids ... jects to the sounds ... celebrations. The new ... ed and inaugurated wit...

BACKSTAGE

Film tourism is a growing phenomenon, once fuelled by the western films set in the country's national parks, today sparked by the fantasy series "Game of Thrones". Fans from around the world flock to Dalmatia and especially Dubrovnik, a main filming location. With its historic fortifications and authentic medieval flair, it's no surprise that the city was chosen for the fantasy capital of the Seven Kingdoms. Take the opportunity, for one glorious moment, to sit on the Iron Throne on the island of *Lokrum* (see p. 86). Then you can

stroll around the Royal ... Trsteno pretending to ... plotting intrigues. D... to accommodate ... fer tours to the ... restaurant Ko... Game of Th... will surel... ocletia... Kašte... yo...

equally as treacherous. The north-westerly Maestral is said to bring bad weather with high waves and a lot of spray. On the other hand, the Scirocco from the South is not only supposed to blow in sand from the Sahara, but also a depressive mood across the land. In the city-state of Dubrovnik, the wind was once a mitigating factor in the courtroom – offenders were said to receive a milder punishment if the Jugo was blowing at the time they committed their crime. More dangerous than all these winds put together is the dreaded draught. What sounds peculiar is in fact taken deadly seriously in the entire southern Slavic region and every child is warned of its perils. Illnesses, diseases, mood swings, family problems can all be attributed to the fact that two windows were left open and a draught was blowing...

LIVE, BREATHE, EAT FOOTBALL

You may be driving towards Split and suddenly notice the name written on every corner, graffiti-sprayed on every third wall, on the sign above the local baker or printed large on beach towels: Hajduk Split is Croatia's oldest football club, founded in 1911 and worshipped by the locals. The archenemy of every genuine Hajduk fan is Dinamo Zagreb and the legendary rivalry between the two clubs has been known to break out in violence over the years. For this reason, never walk around Dalmatia sporting Dinamo souvenirs unless you're looking for trouble. Hajduk fans, especially the infamous hooligans belonging to the ultra-fan club base Torcida, are reportedly linked to far-right ideologies and are seen wearing T-shirts with the German phrase "Hajduk Jugend" (Hajduk Youth) which has obvious connotations with the Hitler Youth. This fanatical love-hate relationship over football has its limits though: When forest fires raged near Split in the summer of 2017, fans of Hajduk Split and of Dinamo stood side by side to fight the fire.

HIGHLY SKILLED TRIO

Italian Renaissance artists such as Michelangelo are widely known, but few people have probably heard of the names Juraj Dalmatinac, Nikola Firentinac or Andrija Aleši? Right? (We won't tell anyone if you promise to remember their names from now on!). Yet these architects and sculptors are in fact the ambassadors of the Dalmatian Renaissance. In Venetian times, Dalmatia was dominated by Gothic architecture and if the conservative councillors had had it their way in the 14th and 15th century, it would have stayed this way. They rejected point blank the ideas of the rebellious youth and the new emerging style – that was until this trio set the Renaissance movement rolling in Dalmatia with their Italian, humanistic influences. The Dalmatian trademark is an eclectic mixture of old and new, Gothic and other styles influenced by the Renaissance. As his Italian name Giorgio da Sebenico (1410–1475) indicates, he came from Šibenik; however he began his career in Venice where he worked on the Scuola di San Marco, among other projects. In Dalmatia he designed multiple palaces and the cathedral altar in Split, the cathedral in Šibenik (in front of which stands his monument), and the fortifications of Dubrovnik. His colleague, the Tuscan Nikola Firentinac (Niccolò di Giovanni Fiorentino, 1418–1506), imported the style of his homeland to Dalmatia and collaborated with Dalmatinac on Šibenik Cathedral. He may have introduced Dalmatinac to Renaissance ideas in the first place. A frequent third collaborator on significant projects was Andrija Aleši (Andrea Alessi, 1425–1505), a prodigiously talented sculptor from Albania, whose best-known works include the side chapel in Trogir Cathedral – a joint effort with Firentinac. The works of these three masters dominate the architectural landscape of towns in Dalmatia even today.

VIRUS-FREE ZONE

It's a well-known fact that the spotted 101 dogs from the famous Disney film got their name from Dalmatia. But did you know that the word quarantine was also coined here at a time when Dalmatia as it stands today did not yet exist and the autonomous city-state of Dubrovnik (then known as Ragusa) was one of the most important trading and shipping posts in the South. As such, its citizens were exposed to all types of viruses and diseases from around the world. In the battle against the Plague in the 14th century, the first quarantine camps were set up in Dubrovnik to contain the rapid spread of the Black Death. The word "quarantine" comes from the Italian word *quaranta* for "quaranta giorni", meaning forty days, the period that all ships were required to be isolated in camps, one of which was known as *lazareti,* before passengers and crew could go ashore. The lazareti building in Dubrovnik still stands today, not as a hospital but an exhibition venue for local artists.

LONG LIVE THE KING

We are living in the 21st century and the whole of Croatia is a Democratic Republic. The whole of Croatia you say? Think again! One single village on the island Iž is populated by a group of loyalist Dalmatians who refuse to relinquish the monarchy. Located between Dugi otok and Ugljan, this small island off the coast of Zadar clings to its tradition of appointing a new king every year at the end of July. At this folk festival, known as *Iški kralj,* last year's king and his entourage are sailed into the harbour of Veli Iž. The king then bids farewell to his loyal subjects to the sounds of fireworks, bells and celebrations. The new king is then elected and inaugurated with performances

BACKSTAGE

Film tourism is a growing phenomenon, once fuelled by the western films set in the country's national parks, today sparked by the fantasy series "Game of Thrones". Fans from around the world flock to Dalmatia and especially Dubrovnik, a main filming location. With its historic fortifications and authentic medieval flair, it's no surprise that the city was chosen for the fantasy capital of the Seven Kingdoms. Take the opportunity, for one glorious moment, to sit on the Iron Throne on the island of *Lokrum* (see p. 86). Then you can stroll around the Royal Gardens Arboretum Trsteno pretending to be one of the ladies plotting intrigues. Dalmatia is now geared to accommodate fans: Many operators offer tours to the film sets. The Dubrovnik restaurant *Kopun* (see p. 84) even serves a Game of Thrones menu. Fans of the series will surely recognise the vaults in Split's Diocletian's Palace and the towns of Šibenik, Kašteli and Klis. If science fiction is more your cup of tea, then you will be pleased to know that Dubrovnik also appears in "Star Wars VIII."

from choirs, folklore dancers and festivities. The role of king is purely a symbolic one and the ritual is by no means a sign that the islanders wish a return of the Habsburg monarchy or former Croatian kings – the practice goes back to Roman times on the Dalmatian islands. Iž was the only island to hold onto the tradition until the 19th century and revived it in the 1970s as a folkloric festival.

MUSIC FOR THE SOUL

On first listen, the music of Croatia's *klapa* choirs might seem overly sentimental and mawkish; but over time almost everybody eventually falls in love with the magic of these traditional a cappella folk songs, which are played in the background at nearly every restaurant or *konoba*. It doesn't matter if you don't understand the lyrics – they always revolve around sailing, love or the homeland, or a mixture of all three. A respected klapa singer is supposed to make romantic advances to the sea. Fans of klapa music are not really interested in the quality and depth of the lyrics. The word klapa actually means group or community and their lullaby songs invoke a nostalgic image of the Dalmatia of old when the only troubles were catching fish and heartache. Although traditionally it is the men who sing, women and mixed choirs are now standing in the spotlight. The "a cappella singing" is sometimes accompanied by a type of mandolin, known as the *tamburica*. Some of the more famous groups such as *Klapa Intrade* and *Klapa Cambi* from Split have managed to combine the sound of klapa with pop/pop-rock and appear with Croatian pop stars or cover their hits.

BEACH IN SIGHT

A picturesque white beach, a shady spot underneath in the pine trees and

A long piece of fabric started life in Croatia

pebbles under your flip flops: The region's beaches are Dalmatia's gold. The only obstacles being the sharp rugged rocks and sea urchins – but don't panic, simply invest in a pair of wet shoes. And although sea urchins are not high in the popularity stakes, these prickly creatures are a good sign because they are usually found in clean water. Fine pebbly beaches can be tracked down all along the Makarska Riviera yet you will struggle to find real sand anywhere. Anyway between you and me, sandy beaches are overrated. Offshore pebbly beaches, snorkelers and divers are also treated to HD underwater images. Locals as well as the numerous blue flags waving at many beaches vouch for the cleanliness of the Adriatic.

FOOD & DRINK

With the sea on their doorstep, kitchen gardens full of herbs and vegetables, and a down-to-earth Slavic tradition and temperament, Dalmatia couldn't ask for any better ingredients for its cuisine – which is as delicious as it is unpretentious.

The **wafer-thin sliced Dalmatian ham**, *pršut*, simply melts in the mouth, accompanied by the bitter aroma of hard cheese and beautiful golden olives, while the bream or sea bass on your plate was plucked from the ocean by fishermen that very morning. Refined recipes and laborious preparation are unnecessary when the ingredients are so impeccably fresh – which is the case almost everywhere along the Dalmatian coast.

The Dalmatians, like most southern Europeans, aren't big on breakfast. They are happy with a cup of coffee. It is not until the *marenda*, the second breakfast, served in late morning, an early lunch break, when many cafés sell cheap **hearty small plates** such as *rižot, njoki, girice* or *pašticada.* On Sundays and public holidays the *marenda* is extended into a lavish feast with multiple courses – and understandably followed by a siesta. A lighter meal is then served in the evening, such as a cold plate of starters, salad or a soup.

Naturally, Croatians have adapted to fit in with tourist schedules, and you can generally choose any dish from the menu both during the day and in the evening. The most commonly available dishes are **pasta and risotto**

Slow food is no trend here – Dalmatian cuisine has always been prepared with a great deal of time and care

together with the most popular (and on hot days the most digestible) starter of *pršut,* cheese and olives. Risottos are made with many different ingredients, and the most popular variations are *črni rižot,* which is coloured black with cuttlefish ink; *rižot s lignjama* with squid; and *rižot s gljivama* with mushrooms. Dalmatia has relatively few typical main courses, the principal ones being *pašticada* – a type of stewed meat – and lamb cooked with ***aromatic herbs*** in a *peka. Čevapčiči* – grilled rolls

of minced meat originating from Bosnia – are also very popular. The majority of main courses involve grilled meat or fish, deliciously seasoned with fresh herbs such as rosemary or thyme, garlic and ***naturally pure olive oil.*** When ordering, remember that fish is almost always sold based on its weight, with prices ranging from 300 to 500 kuna per kilo depending on the quality – so make sure you specify how many grams of fish you want to eat. White bread is normally offered free of charge. Veg-

ajvar – spicy paste made of red peppers, served with grilled meat

arancini – candied bitter orange peel, a speciality of Dubrovnik

blitva – Swiss chard cooked with garlic and potatoes and served as an accompaniment to meat or fish

brodet – stew from different types of fish

čevapčići – grilled minced meat rolls made from pork and beef, and occasionally with lamb (photo right)

Dalmatinski pršut – air-dried prosciutto

duveč – rice meat, usually with vegetables

fritule – deep-fried yeast dough, dusted with icing sugar

girice – small deep-fried fish, to be eaten whole

janjetina – lamb, often prepared in a *peka*

lozovaca and travarica – grape and herb schnapps

njoki – gnocchi, or potato dumplings

palačinke – pancakes with a jam or chocolate sauce

paški sir – sheep's cheese from the island of Pag (photo left)

pašticada – braised beef; dried figs lend the sauce a sweet flavour

peka – a lidded iron pan which is placed directly in the coals of an oven, generally used to cook lamb, fish or poultry with vegetables

pljeskavica – grilled minced steak, sometimes stuffed with cheese, *kajmak*

rižot – risotto, prepared with seafood, mushrooms or meat depending on the season

rožata – créme caramel from Dubrovnik, usually served wirh *arancini*

salata od hobotnice – squid salad

etables are often limited to Swiss chard, which is heavily seasoned with garlic and cooked with potatoes; or you can order a *crisp mixed salad* instead. When it comes to desserts there is generally not a lot of choice, the standard offerings being pancakes or ice cream. Gourmets on the hunt for refined recipes may have long viewed Dalmatia as a culinary wasteland, yet in recent years increased awareness of regional ingredients and recipes has led top chefs to discover **domestic delicacies** such as truffles from Istria, cheese from the island of Pag, oysters from Ston or salt from the lagoon in Nin. For example: Rudolf Štefan of *Pelegrini* (see p. 40) in Šibenik serves his mussels in home-pressed cider with leek and bacon, while his beef cheek stewed with wild herbs from the Velebit mountains approaches perfection. Hrvoje Tomičić of *Kod Kapetana* (see p. 58) in Hvar persuaded his grandmother to share her recipe for *pećicu u tećicu* – a well-nigh forgotten traditional dessert made from goat's cheese, milk and sugar –and honed it for a modern audience. **Croatian sashimi**, or finely sliced raw fish, can be found on many menus nowadays – as can Croatian tapas, in which the well-known starter plate takes on a more refined form.

The food is accompanied by mineral water *(gazirana* for sparkling, *negazirana* for still), Croatian beer (*Ožujsko* and *Karlovačko* are the most popular native brands), or a glass of wine. Given the presence of large wine-growing areas and many **top vintners** wine connoisseurs will be keen to sample the many fine products, which are also often served by the glass. Dalmatia is home to the varieties *Dingač* (Pelješac), *Plavac* (Korčula) and *Babić* (Primošten). On Brač you can also savour a superb rosé: *Spoža,* from the *Senjković* cellar, has been named one of the best in Croatia. The alcohol content of Dalmatian wines is generally around 12%, while the schnapps that rounds off a generous meal is of course a little stronger – just be careful when tasting the home-distilled varieties!

Vegetarians and vegans will generally struggle to find suitable fare. But the trend is moving, albeit slowly, to plant-based cooking: Especially in larger towns and cities there are now restaurants that cook without meat.

Whether you eat in a *konoba* (a folkloric extension of a rustic wine cellar), in one of the many mid-price restaurants that can be found on the shoreline promenades, or in a fine dining venue, you will almost invariably be served with **authentic Dalmatian cuisine**. Most restaurants in tourist hot spots open continuously from lunchtime until late in the evening, and in the high season they are generally open seven days a week.

You can also find pleasant dining spots away from the shoreline promenades

SHOPPING

The blue-and-white striped towels, sun hats and baskets sold by the Croatian-Slovenian chain *Aqua* are simply enchanting, and encapsulate the Mediterranean lifestyle. Branches can be found in every holiday resort. Unusual souvenirs are unfortunately uncommon in Dalmatia. The souvenirs available here are still typical of tourist destinations. That is why your best bet is "back to nature", because the regional products are unrivalled!

ART

Many artists live and work in Dalmatia. One of them is *Ive Kora (www.ivekora. com)* in Postira on Brač, whose sculptures carved out of olive wood have an incredibly sensuous feel. With a bit of luck you will be able to find a gallery with works by local artists in almost every Dalmatian town.

HONEY

Dalmatian herbs and scented maquis produce the perfect conditions for lots of differently flavoured honeys. The island of Hvar has lavender-flavoured honey. Honey, like oil, is sold at markets and at the side of the road by the producers. At the market you can also find Dubrovnik's speciality *arancini:* bitter orange peels that are preserved by being candied.

LACE DOILIES & FILIGREE JEWELLERY

Each region has its own method for making lace doilies, which can be woven, crocheted or embroidered. However they are produced, they make attractive souvenirs – just make sure that there isn't a "Made in China" label hidden on it before you buy! Filigree jewellery also has a long tradition in Dalmatia and was probably taken over from the Ottomans. Most of the silver and gold items available today are not of particularly good quality. Since they are sold at relatively inexpensive prices, they still make for a nice, local souvenir.

LAVENDER

When the lavender fields are in bloom on Hvar, the entire island is immersed in the scent of this aromatic, moth-repellent herb. Lavender can be bought in a small pouch or in bulk, as an oil or as a soap or bath product.

Fleur de sel, award-winning olive oil, fancy schnapps – culinary souvenirs are always popular

MUSIC

You will see: as soon as you have heard one of the mournful polyphonic Dalmatian songs, this gentle, melancholy music will not let you go anymore. A CD of one of the famous *klapa* choirs will let you take a bit of the Dalmatian attitude towards life home with you.

OLIVE OIL

Producers often sell their cold-pressed oil by the side of the road or at the market. Sometimes they refine it with herbs such as rosemary or with garlic. Tourist information centres will be able to tell you where you can get truly pure oil. It is also available in supermarkets. The brand *Zvijezda* has a particularly good reputation!

SALT

Sea salt has been obtained in Dalmatia through the process of evaporation since time immemorial. It is a pure and healthy natural product. Coarse and fine sea salt as well as "fleur de sel", "flower of salt", is available in supermarkets or directly from the salt pans in Nin or Ston.

WINE & SCHNAPPS

The red wines of the Pelješac peninsula are available in every supermarket. It is, of course, much more fun to taste them at the vineyard and choose them there. Along Pelješac's wine route there are several establishments offering tastings.

When it comes to schnapps, it is best to beware of home brew. Although it is offered as a particular speciality, it is often of lesser quality. The grappa-like *lozovaca*, the aromatic *travarica* (herbal schnapps) or the rare *rogač*, obtained from the fruits of the carob tree, should be bought from specialist suppliers or from a well-known producer.

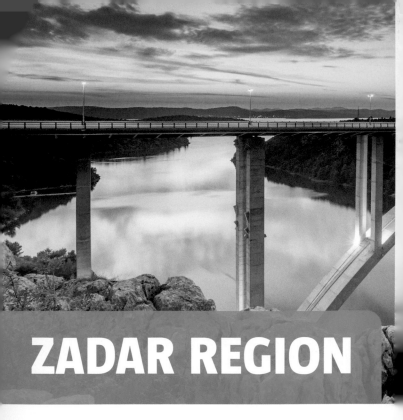

ZADAR REGION

The North Dalmatian coast – running from the Velebit mountains in the north to the fishing village Primošten on a peninsula in the south – is one of Croatia's most fascinating landscapes, lined with countless islands and rocky crags.

Fishermen say of the Kornati archipelago that God shed tears over the inhospitable coastline, and that these tears were transformed into islands. In reality, it was the sea that flooded this hilly landscape after the last ice age until only the limestone ridges were left jutting from the water. Natural wonders and artistic treasures lie close together in the north of Dalmatia: from the proud port cities of Zadar and Šibenik with their Romanesque churches and Renaissance

palaces to the bubbling cascades of the Krka National Park, the canyons of the Paklenica that cut deeply into the Velebit mountains, the delightful olive groves of Ugljan and the cliffs of Dugi otok.

You can find detailed descriptions of Krka and Paklenica National Parks in the third Discovery Tour (see p. 106).

BIOGRAD NA MORU

(139 D5) (*E4*) **Thanks to its role as a point of departure for ferries to Pašman and tours through the Kornati archipelago, this city of 6,000 inhabitants and two marinas is a lively**

Photo: Arch bridge over the Krka river

Turquoise water, a coast with spectacular rocky island landscapes and architectural delights

hub for traffic to the islands during the summer.

The entire *Biograd Riviera* is full of beautiful beaches and comfortable hotels and campsites, and Biograd na Moru and its neighbours *Sv. Filip i Jakov* and *Pakoštane* are popular seaside resorts. Visitors flock to Biograd for its beautiful coves, pine forests and promenade, but the only sights worth seeing in this town that was the seat of the Croatian kings in the 11th century are the museum and the small old town around the 18th century Sv. Stošije church.

SIGHTSEEING

CITY MUSEUM ●

Well worth a visit on a rainy day: The core of the collection is the **INSIDER TIP** cargo of a Venetian ship that sank off Pašman in the 16th century. *Mon–Fri 8am–2pm, 4pm–8pm, Sat 9am–noon | 10 kuna | Kralja Petra Krešimira IV 20 | www.muzej-biograd.com*

Biograd's harbour is a point of departure for trips into the Kornati archipelago

FOOD & DRINK

CARPYMORE
A favourite among the many restaurants on the promenade offering Mediterranean and Italian cuisine. Also rooms with breakfast *(Moderate)*. *Kralja Tvrtka 10 | tel. 023 38 61 19 | www.carpymore.hr | Moderate–Expensive*

CASA VECCHIA
In this secluded old town courtyard, you can enjoy the taste of pizza and pasta under the shade of the trees. *Kralja Kolomana 30 | tel. 023 38 32 20 | Moderate*

SPORTS & BEACHES

The main beach, *Dražica,* is popular with families thanks to its fine, gently sloping shingle, a saltwater pool and waterslides. *Soline* is another shady and sandy beach ideal for children. *Crvena Luka* bay to the south is also fringed with sand and offers numerous activities including inflatable water parks, parasailing and jet skiing.

The diving centre *Albamaris (at Dražica beach | albamaris.hr)* takes guests on excursions to the Kornati National Park to dive down to a ship's wreck and other underwater highlights.

ENTERTAINMENT

Bars line up along the promenade, the Riva, serving cocktails. If clubbing is your thing, head to the sandy beach of *Soline.*

LAVENDER BED BAR
Relax on comfortable loungers with a cocktail. The bar of the Adriatic hotel, decorated in purple, is Biograd's hotspot. *Daily until 1am | Tina Ujevića 7*

WHERE TO STAY

CRVENA LUKA
This modern luxury hotel is part of a resort of villas and apartments. *45 rooms | Crvena Luka 1 | 3 km/1.9 miles south | tel. 023 38 36 40 | www.crvena-luka.hr | Expensive*

PALMA
This quiet family-run guesthouse is located at the edge of town, around 400 m/1,310 ft away from the beach. *20 rooms | Vlahe Bukovca 3 | tel. 023 38 44 63 | Moderate*

BOAT CONNECTIONS

Ferries depart to *Tkon* on the island of *Pašman* several times a day *(www.jadrolinija.hr)*. A number of travel agencies organise boat trips into the *Kornati archipelago* or the *Telašćica Nature Park* on the southern tip of the island *Dugi otok*.

INFORMATION

Tourist information (Trg hrvatskih velikana 2 | tel. 023 38 31 23 | www.tzg-biograd.hr)

WHERE TO GO

MURTER AND THE KORNATI ARCHI-PELAGO (138–139 C–D 5–6) *(Ω E–F4)*
The 148 islands and rocky outcrops that make up the ⭐ *Kornati archipelago* are sprinkled along the coast between Biograd na Moru and the island of Murter. The true beauty of the islands can only be seen from the sea (permits to enter the National Park cost upwards of 300 kuna per day), travelling by boat around the islands. On the island of *Ravni Žakan,* for example, the *Konoba Žakan (tel. 091 3 77 60 15 | Expensive)* serves freshly caught fish to its guests. Or if you choose to dine at the *Konoba Levrnaka (tel. 091 4 35 37 77 | Moderate)* on the island of the same name, you can follow your meal with a dip in crystal-clear waters on the only sandy beach in the whole archipelago. You can also explore the Kornati islands by kayak, on a mountain bike or with a snorkel. A special treat: `INSIDER TIP ▶` kayak tours combined with yoga or bee-keeping classes or dolphin watching tours, organised by *Malik Adventures (tel. 091 784 75 47 | www.malikadventures.com)*.
Information: *Tourist Info (Rudina | tel. 022 43 49 95 | www.tzo-murter.hr)*
Ships for excursions to the national park lie at anchor in almost every coast-

al town; most of them setting off from the island of *Murter,* in the main village of the same name (2,000 inhabitants). This rustic island is dotted with holiday apartments and small campsites. Overnight visitors can find comfortable rooms and tasty fare at the guesthouse *Gina (13 rooms | Put Jazine 9 | Tisno | tel. 022 43 85 80 | Moderate)* and can visit *Zameo ih vjetar (Hrvatskih vladara 5 | tel. 022 43 44 75 | Moderate)* to try the pizza speciality *bubbizza.*
Information: *Nacionalni Park Kornati (Butina 2 | Murter | tel. 022 43 57 42 | www.kornati.hr)*

PAKOŠTANE AND LAKE VRANA (139 D5) *(Ω F4)*
The attractive old town of *Pakoštane* (2,000 inhabitants) lies 6 km/3.7 miles southeast of Biograd. Its charms only re-

---

MARCO POLO HIGHLIGHTS

⭐ **Kornati archipelago**
Where God's tears created a magical landscape → p. 35

⭐ **Telašćica Nature Park**
A bay with an imposing rock face defying the sea → p. 38

⭐ **Sv. Jakov Cathedral**
The masterpiece of the architect Juraj Dalmatinac in Šibenik → p. 39

⭐ **Vineyards of Primošten**
Thriving vines on rocky hillsides → p. 42

⭐ **Zadar sea organ**
Listen to the music of the waves → p. 45

⭐ **Sv. Donat and Sv. Stošija**
Two unusual churches in Zadar → p. 46

veal themselves as you wander through the lanes or stop for a break in one of the cafés on the seafront, where you can gain a sense of the atmosphere of the former fishing village whose pious inhabitants gave the names "Faith", "Hope" and "Love" to the three small islands offshore. Pakoštane is a popular bathing spot among families thanks to its gently sloping sand/shingle beaches such as *Punta* and *Janice*. Windsurfing, kayaking and catamaran trips are offered by *Galeb Adventures (Obala Krešimira 72 | tel. 091 5 42 39 02 | www.galebaventures.com)*. You can also rent a **INSIDER TIP** Zodiac dinghy and explore the Kornati archipelago.

Retreat from the hustle and bustle to the inner courtyard of the *Konoba Pakoštanac (Kraljice Jelene 23 | tel. 023 38 24 73 | Budget)* and dine on richly spiced grilled meat under olive trees.

Information: *Tourist Info (Kraljice Jelene 78 | tel. 023 38 18 92 | www.pako stane.hr)*

Just 1 km/0.6 mile away lies *Lake Vrana (Vransko jezero)*, where at the reserve at the northern end of the nature park *(admission 20 kuna)* you can spot not just the crows that gave the lake its name *(vrana = crow)*, but also great white egrets, purple herons, merlin and marsh harriers. A cycle path of 40 km/25 miles runs round the lake (bike rental at the 11th-century fortress and the Ottoman caravanserai *Maškovica Han (www. maskovicahan.hr)* (built in 1644/1645) are a reminder of turbulent times. Accomodation, restaurant and a small museum. The view from 250 m/820 ft high ᗡᐧᒫ *Kamenjak* hill of the lake, the coastline and the Kornati islands surrounded by the blue of the sea is fantastic.

Information: *Park prirode Vransko jezero (Kralja Petra Svačića 2 | Biograd na Moru | tel. 023 38 31 81 | vransko-jezero.hr)*

DUGI OTOK

(138 B–C 4–5) (*D–E 3–4*) **The 52 km/32 miles-long Dugi otok ("long island") is only 4 km/2.5 miles across at its widest point, and runs like a rod before Zadar, cutting the archipelago off from the open sea beyond it.**

Although its north end is green with olive groves and copses, the landscape changes its countenance as you travel down the island's only road, culminating in the *Telašćica Nature Park* with its karst features. Here on the island's southernmost tip, the landscape boasts an almost otherworldly beauty, and if you sail a boat into the natural harbour of Telašćica bay you will enjoy a magnificent view of the sheer and rugged rocky cliffs.

Only around 2,400 people live on Dugi

otok; its tourist infrastructure is chiefly located in the south in the island's main village of *Sali* (pop. 750), and in *Božava* (pop. 160) in the north-west. Mountain bikers will relish the rather steep ● ☀ *panoramic road* that runs from north to south, with stunning views over the sea and the islands. You can pick up a cycle map from the tourist information centre in Sali, and bikes can be rented from the *Gelateria Conteš (Porat 1 | tel. 098 331184 | www.contes.hr)* in Sali *(mountain bike approx. 200 kuna/day, branch in Božava)*. Climbers will find routes in **INSIDER TIP** *Stara kava,* a disused quarry between the villages of Luka and Savar in the middle of the island.

PLACES ON DUGI OTOK

BOŽAVA (138 B4) (*m* D3)

The houses lining the deep and sheltered cove of *Božava* (pop. 160) couldn't exactly be called picturesque, but the village makes a great base for trips to hidden rocky coves, as well as to the famous sandy beach *Sakarun* 3 km/1.9 mile away. It is also close to the north-western tip of the island, where the *Veli rat lighthouse* has cast its signal out across the Adriatic since 1849. You can climb the tower's over 200 steps if you ask the lighthouse keeper. The small campsite *Kargita (50 pitches | Veli rat 67 | tel. 098 53 23 33 | www.camp-kargita.hr | Budget)* is popular with individualists, while for four-star comfort, the hotel *Maxim (30 rooms | tel. 023 29 12 91 | www.hoteli-bozava.hr | Moderate)* lies directly on the coast and is part of the largest hotel complex on the island. The diving school *Božava (tel. 023 31 88 91 | www.bozava.de/eng)* also offers diving trips. Among the few restaurants on the north end of the island, the bistro **INSIDER TIP** *Gorgonia (Verunić | tel. 91 737 98 23 | www.gorgonia.hr | also apartments | Moderate)* is worth the 5 km/3.1 miles journey from Božava. Here, you can sit on the seafront as you savour freshly cooked fish and meat.

Dramatic ending: the spectacular cliff face on the southernmost tip of Dugi otok

SALI (138 C5) (*♢ E4*)

This small village (pop. 750) on the south-eastern coast welcomes its visitors with a view of pastel-coloured facades clustered round a narrow harbour. There have been fishermen based here for over 1,000 years. The only hotel, *Sali (48 rooms | tel. 023 37 70 49 | www.hotel-sali.hr | Moderate)* on Sašćica bay, offers its guests an attractive shingle beach and plenty of sporting activities, while

An admission charge *(40 kuna)* is payable at the *office of the park authority;* from this point you will need to walk (or sail) around 2 km/1.2 mile to the ● *salt lake Mir*, whose waters are ideal for bathing – and significantly warmer than the sea. A INSIDER TIP spectacular view can be found at the end of the ten-minute climb from the nature park office up to the clifftop on the western coast: ⚞ *Kliff Grpašćak* features an al-

Šibenik's old town with a view of the cathedral

the restaurant *Špageritimo (tel. 023 37 72 27 | Expensive)* has made a name for itself with its creative fish dishes.

TELAŠĆICA NATURE PARK ★
(138 C5) (*♢ E4*)

Just under 9 km/5.6 miles to the south of Sali begins the *Park (www.telascica.hr)*, which comprises the deep, south-facing Telašćica bay, its 13 rocky islets, and the cliff face with which Dugi otok's south-western coast rises above the Adriatic. Countless boats rest at anchor in the sheltered waters of the bay.

most vertical drop of over 160 m/525 ft into the sea. From April until October, Goran opens the doors of his konoba *Go Ro (tel. 098 85 34 43 | Expensive)* on the bay. The fish is caught by Goran himself or by his friends, the vegetables are grown in the garden.

BOAT CONNECTIONS

Car ferries connect *Zadar* to *Brbinj* several times a day; there are also hydrofoil departures from *Zadar* to *Božava*. Information: *www.jadrolinija.hr*

TOURIST INFO
Obala Petra Lorinja | Sali | tel. 023 37 70 94 | www.dugiotok.hr

ŠIBENIK

(140 B2) (*ⓜ F–G4*) **Behind the dreary suburbs of Dalmatia's third-largest port (pop. 47,000) hides a meandering old town, dotted with Renaissance Palaces and brought to life by young street musicians. Festivals are held back to back in the town over summer ranging from jazz *(OFF Jazz & Blues Festival)*, alternative music *(Regius)* to bass *(Membrain)* so make sure to enquire which concerts are on during your stay. *www.sibenik-tourism.hr/en/town-of-festivals***

The Unesco World Heritage Site of the cathedral *Sv. Jakov* stands on a terrace above the waterfront promenade and dominates the city's skyline with its white marble dome. The splendid palaces in the tangle of streets surrounding it and leading up to the ☀ ruins of Fort *Sv. Mihovil* (13th–18th centuries) act as a reminder of Šibenik's long history: the city on the Krka estuary was founded by Croatian kings in the 11th century.

Šibenik is an ideal base for touring the nearby Šibenik archipelago, with its main islands of *Krapanj* and *Prvić*, and the *Kornati archipelago.* In the hinterland, footpaths and waterways wind between the cascades of the River Krka in the National Park of the same name (see p. 109).

(see p. 109)

SIGHTSEEING

OLD TOWN
The main artery is the *Ulica kralja Tomislava,* which has staircases branching off from it. It ends in the *Trg Republike Hrvat-*

ske (Square of the Croatian Republic) with its unique collection of buildings: the *Cathedral,* the 16th-century *Loggia* with its wide-arched arcade, and the neighbouring *City Hall (Gradska vijećniva).* The 15th-century *Rector's Palace (Knežev palač)* was used as a residence by the newly appointed dukes at the beginning of Venetian rule, and is today home to the *City Museum (Mon–Fri 8am–8pm, Sat/Sun 10am–8pm | 30 kuna | Gradska vrata 3 | www.muzej-sibenik.hr)* which offers a modern exhibition on the history of the city. The *Dalmatinac Monument* on the square commemorates the architect of the cathedral. The four 15th century well shafts on the neighbouring *Trg 4 Bunara* mark the spot of an underground cistern which was once used to store water in the event of drought and besiegement. The medieval garden belonging to the *St. Lovre Franciscan Monastery (Kačićeva 11 | free admission)* is an inviting oasis hidden away in the old town.

The two smallest attractions lie in the *Ulica kralja Tomislava* and demonstrate the town's love of animals: dogs and cats have congregated here since the 16th century to quench their thirst in summer with the water held in the stone troughs.

SV. JAKOV CATHEDRAL ★

The city's cathedral is considered the masterpiece of the architect Juraj Dalmatinac, who worked on it from 1441 onwards. He took the existing Gothic structure and added a transept and a crossing dome to expand it into a bright Renaissance work made exclusively of stone, demonstrating his technical mastery in the process. His skill can be seen particularly clearly in the INSIDER TIP baptistery, whose dome is made up of nine interlocking stone slabs decorated with reliefs. The 74 portrait heads were designed to commemorate prominent citizens, and show that Dalmatinac had an eye for details. His apprentice Nikola Firentinac completed it in 1535. *Daily, in the summer 8:30am–8pm, in the winter 8:30am–noon, 4–8pm | 15 kuna*

FOOD & DRINK

In the old town there are a number of bars and cafés. In the summer there are often few free spaces.

GRADSKA VIJEĆNICA

The view of the cathedral alone means that you should come here for a drink at the very least; but a dinner under the Renaissance arcades is romantic too, and the food is very good! *Trg Republike Hrvatske 3 | tel. 022 2136 05 | Moderate*

PELEGRINI ☆

The best restaurant in Dalmatia is not far from the cathedral and boasts a view of the sea. The creative Dalmatian cuisine served here offers an elaborate take on traditional dishes. *Closed Mon | Jurja Dalmatinca 1 | tel. 022 2137 01 | Expensive*

VINO I INO

Wine bar serving a range of cold starters and tasty snacks. The wine selection is impressive, and there is often live jazz in the evening – a truly relaxed spot. *Fausta Vrančića | tel. 091 2 50 60 22 | Moderate*

SHOPPING

OGGI BIJOUX

Martina Morić loves colour, and combines strips of leather with Swarovski crystals and plastic bracelets with Murano glass for her pieces. Her jewellery is hip and Mediterranean. *Branitelja Domovinskog rata 2d | oggibijoux.com*

SPORTS & ACTIVITIES

NEXTBIKE ŠIBENIK ⊛

Bicycles and e-bikes are the ideal way to get to local beaches, and are available in multiple locations. They cost 8 kuna an hour to hire. Although you pay a membership fee of 79 kuna when you register by app or online, you get the equivalent free hours on a bike. *www.nextbike.hr*

ENTERTAINMENT

INSIDER TIP ▶ AZIMUT

Located directly underneath the well square, this underground venue in a former cistern is where the town's alternative scene meets up for concerts, exhibitions and theatre under its brick arches. *Mon–Fri 9am–4am, Sat 10am–4am, Sun 9am–1am | Obala palih omladinaca 2*

PUBLIC BAR

This is where Šibenik's young people come together to party and to dance. *Daily until 4am | Bana Josipa Jelačića 2*

WHERE TO STAY

HOSTEL MARE

Stylish and modern hostel on the edge of the old town with air conditioning and free WiFi as standard. *1 double room, 6 dorms | Kralja Zvonimira 40 | tel. 022 2152 69 | hostel-mare.com | Budget*

SHABBY CHIC APARTMENTS

English nostalgia in the heart of the old town, with floral wallpaper, varnish and everything else you might expect. Magical. *2 apartments | Stjepana Radića 7 | tel. 098 33 79 55 | Moderate*

SOLARIS BEACH RESORT

The holiday complex on a peninsula south-west of the town consists of hotels, apartment villas and a campground. Nice pebble and sand beaches, many sporting activities with spa centre and the *Solaris Aquapark*. Also INSIDER TIP▸ Nordic Walking tours to the *Sv. Nikola fortress. 1,300 rooms | Hotelsko naselje Solaris | tel. 022 36 0 01 | www.solaris.hr | Budget–Expensive*

BOAT CONNECTIONS

Car ferry twice daily from *Šibenik* to *Zlarin, Kaprije* and *Žirje* in the Šibenik archipelago, foot passenger ferry several times daily to *Zlarin, Prvić Luka, Šepurine* and *Vodice.*

INFORMATION

TOURIST INFO
Obala palih omladinaca 3 | tel. 022 21 44 11 | www.sibenik-tourism.hr

WHERE TO GO

BRODARICA AND KRAPANJ
(140 A–B2) (*ഈ F4*)
Despite its many hotels and restaurants, *Brodarica* (pop. 2,500, 6 km/3.7 miles to the south) is still a quiet holiday destination. The *Zlatna Ribica* restaurant *(Krapanjskih spužvara 46 | tel. 022 35 06 95 | Moderate)* is popular for its fish dishes and has wonderful guest rooms as well *(27 rooms, 3 bungalows)*. There is an hourly ferry to the island of *Krapanj,* but you could just swim across to it, as it only lies 300 m/985 ft away from shore. The island is home to sponge divers, who still perform their dangerous work today. Krapanj is a worthwhile diving destination for visitors too, and the owner of the hotel *Spongiola (18 rooms, 5 apartments | Obala I 58 | tel. 022 34 89 00 | www. spongiola.com | Expensive)* can recommend the best locations to you.

Pelegrini restaurant – serving the finest cuisine outdoors

Information: *Tourist Info (Krapanj spužvara 1 | tel. 022 35 06 12 | www.tz-broda rica.hr)*

SV. NIKOLA FORTRESS (140 A2) (*ഈ F4*)
The impressive bastion appears to be floating on the sea at the entrance to the St. Anthony Channel. Croatia's latest World Heritage Site (2017) was built in the 16th century to protect Šibenik from the open sea. You can reach the fort over a small island along a narrow route which crosses the channel.

OBONJAN ⊛ (140 A2) (*ഈ F4*)
This tiny, "adult-only" island is the place to find your Zen. This destination promises the ultimate in relaxation where you

The winegrowers in Primošten are known for cultivating their babić grapes on stony soil

can practice yoga, go snorkelling and enjoy a smoothie at the green bar – a paradise even for vegans. The stone-walled amphitheatre provides DJs with the perfect stage at night. Accommodation is in luxury safari-type tents with proper beds and air-conditioning. Three ferries leave Šibenik daily for the island *(approx. 40 min., 150 Kuna return)* or you can take a private boat taxi *(approx. 25 min., prices depend on number of passengers and season, www.obonjan-boat.com)* | *Moderate–Expensive*

PRIMOŠTEN (140 B3) *(🕮 F5)*

Situated on a teardrop-shaped island, the houses of the old town in this picturesque holiday village (pop. 1,500) cluster around the *Sv. Juraj church* (15th century) that sits enthroned on its hill. A causeway connects Primošten to the modern suburbs and hotel complexes on the mainland, while the *Raduča* peninsula with its thick pine forest and 800 m/2,625 ft-long shingle beach lies opposite. Stroll through the town past souvenir shops and cafés until you reach the ⚲ *parish church* and its quiet cemetery, which offers a beautiful view of the sea and the mainland. The ★ ⚲ *vineyards of Primošten* are actually slopes covered with rock, with small patches left clear that offer just enough room for a vine to grow. The soil is therefore protected against corrosion from wind and water and the heat stored in the stone by day is used to keep the grapes warm at night. This results in the *Babić* red wine, which you can sample at the agro-tourism company ⚲ INSIDER TIP *Baćulov Dvor (Primošten Burnji | www.baculov-dvor. com | Moderate)* located 7 km/4.3 miles to the north-east. Here, you can also try homegrown organic herbs, oil and honey.

Information: *Tourist Info (Trg biskupa Josipa Arnerića 2 | tel. 022 57 11 11 | www. tz-primosten.hr)*

VODICE AND PRVIĆ (140 A2) *(〽 F4)*

The small town of *Vodice* (pop. 6,700) 15 km/9.3 miles to the north of Šibenik is one of the most popular holiday destinations on the Dalmatian coast thanks to its shingle beaches – including the famous "Blue Beach" *Plava plaža* – and is also a hot spot for clubbing holidays. The club *Aurora (July–Sept | Kamenar 3 | www.auroraclub.hr)* stays open all night long, and features performances by Croatian stars and DJs.

If you need to get away from the crowds then make a trip to the island of *Prvić (passenger ferries: www.jadrolinija.hr)*. The picturesque villages of *Prvić Luka* and *Šepurine* are only a ten-minute walk from each other, and the shingle beaches along the way will invite you to take a dip in the crystal-clear sea. The ● *Memorijalni centar Faust Vrančić (mainly Mon–Fri 9am–4pm, July/Aug Mon–Sat 9am–8pm | 30 kuna | Ulica 1a | Prvić Luka)* exhibits more than 50 wooden models built by the first ever inventor to test a parachute – way back in the 16th century. If you want to spend the night: the *Hotel Maestral (12 rooms | tel. 022 44 83 00 | www.hotelmaestral.com | Moderate)* is one of the most beautiful places to stay in the region.

Information: *Tourist Info (Obala Vladimira Nazora | tel. 022 44 38 88 | www.vodice.hr)*

UGLJAN AND PAŠMAN

(138–139 B–D 4–5) *(〽 D–E 3–4)*

These two sister islands, covered with lush foliage, can best be explored on panoramic hiking paths or by bike. Let the tranquility soothe you in the many remote monasteries and fishing villages.

The strait separating the two long, narrow islands was only created in 1883, when an isthmus was dug out in order to create a shorter naval route from Zadar to Dugi otok. A bridge was built in the 1970s to connect the islands, which are a popular destination for weekend trips; many people in Zadar own holiday homes here. The accommodation available to holidaymakers generally consists of privately rented rooms and apartments.

PLACES ON UGLJAN

Olive cultivation on *Ugljan* (pop. 7,500, 51 km^2/20 mi^2) dates back to the Roman era, and the olives harvested here in late autumn and winter are used to make one of the best oils in Croatia.

A few historic stone houses and an attractive promenade are the highlights of the village of *Preko,* which is the arrival point for ferries from Zadar. Apart from the ● *public lido* on the promenade, a wide sandy bay invites bathers. There are also several konobas, such as *Konoba Barbara (Put Jerolimovih 4 | tel. 023 28 61 29 | Moderate)* close to the ferry port, where you can order fresh grilled fish. An hour-long walk uphill leads to the ruins of ↯ *Fort Sv. Mihovil* (13th century), which provides a fantastic view over the Zadar archipelago. Holidaymakers are welcome to visit the Franciscan monastery on the island of *Galovac,* and a boat *(5 kuna)* will take you across from the jetty close to the *Tourist Info (Magazin 8 | tel. 023 28 61 08 | www.preko.hr).* Try exploring the neighbouring villages by bicycle: the agency *Nav Travel (Magazin 5 | tel. 023 1 64 35 | navadriatic.com),* offers bike rental, with a mountain bike costing 100 kuna per day, and possible destinations might include the island's main village of *Ugljan* around 10 km/6.2 miles to the north. There, you will find

Confident swimmers can reach the island of Galovac from Preko's beach

a monastery on a pine-forested peninsula, with a sandy beach and shallow waters. A further 2 km/1.2 miles to the north and close to *Muline* lies the idyllic, isolated sandy beach INSIDERTIP ▶ *Vela Luka* – and if you're lucky you might also come across several *Roman archaeological sites* that are open to the public, but difficult to find.

Travel 8 km/5 miles south from Preko along a road running through pine forests and olive groves to reach *Kukljica*. We recommend the *Konoba Stari Mlin* (tel. 023 3733 04 | *Moderate*), whose menu consists mainly of grilled meat and fish. Around 20 minutes' walk away from the village you will find the sand/shingle beach *Sabuša* hidden among pine trees

on the south-western coast, with the *Jelenica* nudist bay a few metres further on. Information: *Tourist Info (Kukljica ulica II 87 | tel. 023 37 32 76 | www.kukljica.hr)*

PLACES ON PAŠMAN

Pašman (pop. 3,500, 57 km²/22 mi²) is also dotted with olive groves and vineyards. An attractive footpath leads you from the main village of *Tkon* up the *Čokovac* hill to the ● *Sv. Kuzma i Damjan monastery (June–Sept Mon–Sat 4–6pm)*.Inside, there is a unique candle holder, which protrudes from the wall in the shape of a human arm.

8 km/5 miles to the north, in *Mrljane*, the sand/shingle beach is so flat that you need to wade a long way out before the water becomes deep enough to swim in. A bumpy 50 km/31 mile ☆ mountain bike track circles the island, offering plenty of great views along the way. Maps are available from the tourist info in Tkon. If you're hungry after all that cycling, sit on the breezy terrace of the restaurant *Lanterna (Pašman | tel. 023 26 0179 | www.lanterna.hr | Moderate)*, where a large variety of freshly caught fish is served.

Information: *Tourist Info (in the harbour | www.tkon.hr)*

BOAT CONNECTIONS

From *Preko* on *Ugljan* to *Zadar* and from *Tkon* on *Pašman* to *Biograd na Moru* several times daily *(www.jadrolinija.hr)*.

ZADAR

▨▨ MAP INSIDE THE BACK COVER
▨▨ (138 C4) *(Ø E3)* **Dalmatia's second-largest port (pop 73,000) preserves three millennia of art and architecture,**

but there are also traces left by the city's more recent history – and here we don't just mean the enchanting art installation of the *Sea Organ* and the *Greeting to the Sun,* where the city's inhabitants gather to watch the sunset.

Zadar's old town lies on a peninsula, connected to the mainland by just one narrow access point. The city was expanded under Venetian rule into a naval fortress from 1409 onwards, complete with walls and towers. Zadar was the capital of Dalmatia until 1918 and its culture was strongly influenced by a large Italian community until 1947, when they left the city after it became part of Yugoslavia. This Italian flair can still be felt today in the city centre, with its many cafés. Amid the Baroque and Gothic houses in the narrow streets of the old town there are plenty of examples of *razionalismo,* the Italian architectural style of the fascist period, which were built during the 1920s and 1930s when Zadar was an Italian exclave. British and American bombing raids destroyed the majority of the old town in 1943/44.

SIGHTSEEING

ARCHAEOLOGICAL MUSEUM (ARHEOLOŠKI MUZEJ) ★

Start at the top and go down again chronologically through Zadar's history – from the Illyrians to the Romans, Slavs and the early Croatian middle ages – is documented in this museum by means of some spectacular exhibits that include sarcophagi, baptismal fonts and shrines dating from the 9th to the 11th centuries. A special section tells of the time when the Romans ruled Dalmatia. The museum shop sells INSIDER TIP▶ handmade jewellery. *July/Aug daily 9am–10pm, June, Sept daily 9am–9pm, April/May, Oct Mon–Sat 9am–3pm, Nov–* *March Mon–Fri 9am–2pm, Sat until 1pm | 40 kuna incl. admission to Sv. Donat | Trg opatice Čike 1 | www.amzd.hr*

GLASS MUSEUM (MUZEJ ANTIČKOG STAKLA)

Playing with fire is fun to watch in this museum where you can see how glass jewellery is moulded from a liquid mass. The well-made replicas of the Roman exhibits such as cups, bowls, perfume bottles and lamps can be purchased in the museum shop. *Mon–Sat 9am–9pm | 30 kuna | Poljana Zemaljskog odbora 1 | www.mas-zadar.hr*

GOLD AND SILVER OF ZADAR (ZLATO I SREBRO ZADRA)

The *Benedictine convent (Mon–Sat 10am–1pm, 5–7pm, Sun 10am–1pm, winter closed Sun | 30 kuna)* shows relics and ecclesiastical treasures from across Dalmatia, decorated with precious stones and filigree.

SEA ORGAN (MORSKE ORGULJE) ★ ●

Zadar's favourite meeting point among natives and tourists alike is the product of a redesign of the harbour on the westernmost tip of the 500 m/1,640 ft wide

---

CITY WHERE TO START?
From the waterfront promenade **Obala kneza Branimira** in the new town (you will find parking here too) a footbridge will take you to the peninsula with the historic town centre. Keep going straight to get to **Narodni trg,** where you will also find the tourist information. However, it is far more romantic to travel across the harbour from the *barjakoli* in a rowing boat (5 kuna) – an 800-year-old tradition.

peninsula. The architect Nikola Basić designed not just the modern ferry terminal, but also a stylish waterfront promenade with steps running down to the sea. Under the steps are a number of plastic tubes of varying length, each with a pipe attached to the end. These pipes produce noises that are sometimes eerie, sometimes contemplative, depending on the rhythm of the waves – and occasionally recalling the song of a whale. Only when the mighty Bora threatens, the holes are closed. The installation is rounded off by the ◉ *Greeting to the Sun (Pozdrav suncu)*. This is a disc made up of 300 glass plates that store energy in their solar cells during the day, before releasing it at night in the form of colourful light signals that are triggered by people's footsteps on the disc. The majority of the power generated is used to power the lights on the shore.

LOW BUDGET

With two of Šibenik's hostels located just next door, the *No. 4 Club (daily from 8am | Trg Dinka Zavorovića 4 | tel. 022 217517)* is both a meeting point for travellers and a good-value eatery offering hearty breakfasts and juicy steaks.

The snack bar *Sardela Snack (Zadarska ulica)* run by the cooperative fishery in Kali on the island of Ugljan serves up freshly grilled sardines and anchovies at unbeatable prices.

The self-service restaurant *Barbakan (Ruđera Boškovića 5 | tel. 023 30 09 70)* in Zadar's former citadel offers good-value food in atmospheric surroundings.

NARODNI TRG

Zadar's "People's Square" is a hub of activity until late in the evening. The central square of the old town is lined with a Baroque *Loggia* (16th century), the *City Guard* building in Renaissance style, and the 19th-century *City Hall.* The foundations of the 11th-century *Sv. Lovro* church are preserved in the *Café Lovre,* and a few steps further on you can see the attractive *Ghirardini Palace* with its Venetian Gothic style.

SV. DONAT AND SV. STOŠIJA ★

From the remnants of columns and temple foundations it is obvious that this square with its two churches used to be a Roman forum. The idiosyncratic rotunda of the *Sv. Donat church (daily 9am–7pm, June 9am–9pm, July/Aug 9am–10pm | 20 kuna)* was built in the 9th century. This pre-Romanesque building is unusually tall, at 26 m/85 ft, and its superb acoustics are put to excellent use during the *music evenings* (see p. 123) held here in the summer. Inside, the remains of Roman columns and capitals are preserved alongside old Croatian reliefs. Zadar's *Sv. Stošija cathedral (summer Mon–Fri 8am–2pm, 5–7pm, Sat/Sun 8am–noon, otherwise Mon–Fri 8am–noon, 6–7pm, Sat/Sun 8am–noon)* next door constitutes a 12th/13th-century expansion of the city's sacred centre. Its Romanesque-Gothic architecture and elegant rose windows are reminiscent of Tuscan churches, while its interior features three naves and lavishly decorated altars. Of these, the altar with the sarcophagus containing the relics of the church's patron St Anastasia is of particular note. This dates from the 9th century and is decorated with interlace ornament and a relief depicting the saint. The 56 m/184 ft-high ◁▷ bell tower *(Mon–Sat, June–Sept 9am–10pm, April,*

May, Oct 10am–5pm | 15 kuna) offers superb views over the old town.

TRG PET BUNARA
(SQUARE OF THE FIVE FOUNTAINS)

In earlier times the only way to reach the peninsula was to cross a drawbridge

BISTRO GOURMET KALELARGA

Modern Dalmatian cuisine served in a design ambience. The wine selection is also very good. *Široka 1 | tel. 023 23 30 00 | www.arthotel-kalelarga.com | Expensive*

Remnants of the Roman forum are still visible in front of the 1,200-year-old Sv. Donat church

and pass through the *Land Gate* (1543), built by Michele Sanmicheli in the form of a triumphal arch and still intact. Behind the gate lies the enchanting *Trg pet bunara* with its five Renaissance wells, beneath which Zadar's largest cistern used to collect rainwater. You can still see parts of the crenellated medieval *City Wall* here, along with a watchtower and two beautiful *Palaces* from the 14th/15th centuries. In the Baroque *Sv. Šimun* church, two angels support the imposing gold and silver sarcophagus of the city's patron St Simeon (14th century). To the northwest of the square lies the lively district of ● INSIDER TIP *Varoš* with numerous small shops and bars.

MALO MISTO

A typical Dalmatian restaurant with a large menu and friendly service. You will see plenty of natives eating here too. *Jurja Dalmatinca 3 | tel. 023 30 18 31 | www.malo-misto.com | Moderate*

INSIDER TIP PET BUNARA

This restaurant close to the Fountain Square offers a romantic atmosphere and creative Dalmatian specialities such as ravioli with scampi, or try the typical local fig sauce *šinjorina smokva*. *Ulica Stratico | tel. 023 22 40 10 | www.petbunara.com | Expensive*

Watch the sun go down and the stars go up at The Garden while sipping on a cocktail

SHOPPING

MARKET (TRŽNICA)

Zadar's lively market sees fruit and vegetable stands arranged between the city wall and Narodni trg, while the nearby *indoor fish market* on the edge of the harbour is where you can inspect the catch of the day. Haggling is not forbidden! *Daily 6am–3pm*

SUPERNOVA CENTAR ●

This shopping centre will set fashionable pulses racing with its selection of international chains from Calzedonia to Zara, alongside a few native Croatian brands. *Daily 9am–9pm | Akcije Maslenica 1*

SPORTS & ACTIVITIES

You can find beaches and coves surrounded by pine trees on the *Borik* peninsula north of the city and its marina.

ADVENTURE PARK

Adventure park close to Zadar with miniature golf, zip-wires, water polo and giant trampolines to entertain young and old. *Daily 10am–6pm | on the road to Petrčane | Kožinska cesta 108 | from 100 kuna | www.adventure-park.hr*

ENTERTAINMENT

There is always something happening in the *Varoš* quarter – for instance in the popular *Caffe Galerija Đina (Varoška 2)* or at *Toni (Mihe Klaića 6)*. If there aren't enough chairs to go round then the pews from *Sv. Mihovil* church are set out on the street.

LEDANA

DJs under the trees at the town's coolest open-air bar in the old town park. The place to go in Zadar to party through to the early hours of the morning. *Perivoj kraljice Jelene Madijevke | www.ledana.hr*

zadarskih pobuna 13 | tel. 023 49 49 50 | www.hotel-bastion.hr | *Expensive*

MR. CHARLES HOSTEL

This stylish and colourfully decorated hostel is situated in the new part of town, making it quieter than the hotels in the historic centre. *2 dorms | Andrije Hebranga 1 | tel. 023 38 07 58 | www.mrcharles hostel.com | Budget*

BOAT CONNECTIONS

There are several ferries per day to the neighbouring islands of *Ugljan, Dugi otok* and *Iž,* depending on the season. The smaller car-free islands are also accessible by passenger ferry from Zadar *(www.jadrolinija.hr, www.gv-line.hr).*

INFORMATION

TOURIST INFO

Mihovila Klaića 1 | tel. 023 316 166 | www. zadar.travel

Ten telephone booths were rescued from extinction in Zadar and transformed into smart hotspots providing information, WiFi as well as bus and parking tickets.

WHERE TO GO

IŽ (138 C4–5) (*ad E3*)

Overgrown with macchia and olive groves, this island (pop. 600) between Ugljan and Dugi otok owes its popularity to the folk festival *Iški kralj* (at the end of July/beginning of August) where an island king is chosen each year. Pottery is a centuries-old tradition in the small town of *Veli Iž,* specimens of which are on display in the *Ethnographical Museum (July/Aug. daily 10am–noon, 7pm–9pm).*

An ideal place for spiritual travellers: ☉ *Korinjak (78 rooms | Veli Iž | tel. 023*

THE GARDEN

Legendary lounge bar with a minimalist design, featuring international DJs and tasty craft beers. The bar also serves something which is severely lacking elsewhere in traditional Dalmatia – vegan snacks. *Daily 10:30am–1:30am | Bedemi zadarskih pobuna | www.thegarden.hr/ the-garden-lounge*

WHERE TO STAY

ART HOTEL KALELARGA

This stylish hotel in the heart of the old town treats its guests to puristic design and a high-quality restaurant. *10 rooms | Majke Margarite 3 | tel. 023 23 30 00 | www.arthotel-kalelarga.com | Moderate*

BASTION

Furnished in elegant dark colours, this boutique hotel is just a few feet away from the sea organ. *28 rooms | Bedemi*

27 70 64 | korinjak.com | Moderate). Here, you will be treated to both vegetarian food and a comprehensive programme of activities ranging from morning yoga sessions to meditative walks and communal singing. The hotel is located directly on the beach and also features a campsite set in a nearby pine forest *(150 pitches | Budget)*. Information: *Tourist Info Zadar | crossing: 1 hr 50 mins from Zadar*

NIN AND ZATON (138 C4) (*Ø E3*)

The small town of *Nin* (pop. 1,500) 15 km/9.3 miles to the north-west has pre-Roman roots. This island settlement is connected to the mainland by two bridges, and used to be a religious centre of the Kingdom of Croatia. The main sights are the *City Gate,* the remains of the *city walls* (15th century) and the ★ *Sv. Križ church*, a superb example of early Christian architecture dating from the 9th century that was used as a coronation venue for seven Croatian kings. Guests at the *Aenona (Ulica Petra Zoranića 2 | tel. 023 26 50 04 | Budget)* can sit in the shady garden opposite the church and enjoy the view as they tuck into pizza, fish and grilled dishes.

Nin is especially proud of the "white gold". The lagoon landscape surrounding Nin has been a site of salt production since Roman times, and even today the 🌍 *Solana Nin* extracts salt using traditional methods and without the aid of additives. There is a small *museum (Mon–Fri 8am–8pm, Sat/Sun 9am–8pm | 35 kuna | Ilirska cesta 7 | www.solananin.hr)* that explains the 1,500-year history of salt extraction, tours lead past evaporation basins and Roman remains. You can also buy salts, delicacies and cosmetics flavoured with rosemary or lavender from the INSIDER TIP *museum shop*. And don't forget to try the *arancini* (orange peel) covered in salty chocolate!

DONKEYS TO THE RESCUE

Before the invention of tractors, donkeys were the main means of transport in the vineyards and olive groves in Dalmatia. The services of these helpful creatures are nowadays no longer required – and some are simply abandoned. However er the *Tribunj Tovar* reserve **(139 E6)** (*Ø F4*) *(at the Tribunj Magistrale | visit by appointment only tel. 091 5 07 73 52 | tribunjtovar@gmail.com)* offers these animals a well-earned place for retirement. More canny entrepreneurs try to earn a living from them as tourist attractions on donkey farms such as *Dar Mar* **(138 C4)** (*Ø E3*) *(Poljaci 2A | Žerava | tel. 023 39 01 23)* in Poljica Brig. Their milk is hailed as the latest super food. On the island of Brač, *Ivo Biočina* **(141 D4)** (*Ø H5*) *(Postira | tel. 021 63 22 00)* uses it to produce a cheese delicacy and reputed aphrodisiac which sells at an amazing 8000 kuna per kilo to the USA. The creatures are also the star of a fun race held every August in *Tribunj* where some of the more stubborn mules refuse to let their riders show them the way. However, they are entitled to their diva-like status in Tribunj which honours this humble creature with a life-size bronze statue. With so much attention, it's no surprise that the donkey appears as a symbol on many of the region's postcards.

The sun still has to work its wonders before the salt in the lakes at Nin is ready for harvest

The sandy lagoon surrounding Nin is perfect for surfers. At *Surfmania Surf & Fly Center (Mid-April–Oct | Ždrijac| tel. 098 91 29 8 18 | www.surfmania.hr)* you can hire equipment for surfing and kitesurfing, and you can sign up for courses to learn the basic techniques. Stand-up paddling is also part of the programme. Don't be surprised if you meet people covered head to toe in black crust at the "Queen's Beach": Mud from Nin's sand lagoons was used as long ago as Roman times for medicinal purposes.

The equally historic town of *Zaton,* just 2 km/1.2 miles away, is nowadays characterised by beach activities, especially by families. All that remains to remind visitors of Zaton's earlier importance as Nin's trading port is the old-Croatian *Sv. Nikolas* church, built on a hill in the 11th century. Holidaymakers can find accommodation in the *Zaton Holiday Resort (593 apartments | Dražnikova 67t | tel. 023 28 02 80 | www. zaton.hr | Budget–Moderate),* and its adjoining *campsite (1,500 pitches).*

Information: *Tourist Info Zaton-Nin (Zadarska cesta 39a | tel. 023 26 54 61 | www. zaton-zd.hr)*

SILBA (138 A–B3) *(▢ D2)*

This 15 km² car-free island (pop. 300) has a wealth of idyllic shingle coves, and the main beach in the village of Silba even boasts a fine sandy base. The 30 m/98 ft-tall *"Tower of Love" (Toretta)* is an unmissable landmark that was erected as a lookout post by a 17th-century captain. Silba's other attraction lies underwater in Pocukmarak cove, where archaeologists have unearthed an early Christian sarcophagus and two stone covers used by later generations as material for a jetty for an ● **INSIDER TIP** *underwater museum.* There's no need for diving equipment – a mask and flippers will suffice. Accommodation only in private rooms or apartments. Boats from Zadar depart several times per day *(www.jadrolinija.hr).*

Information: *Tourist Info (tel. 023 37 00 10 | www.tzsilba.hr)*

SPLIT REGION

With the majestic backdrop of the Bio-kovo mountains and the silhouettes of the islands Brač and Hvar looming be-fore the coast, Central Dalmatia is a place where maritime and alpine envi-ronments sit side by side.

The Roman Emperor Diocletian chose to retire on this richly contrasting coastline, and bequeathed to posterity a palace that developed into the bustling city of Split. Both the city and its smaller neighbour Trogir with its Renaissance buildings com-bine historical architecture with metropol-itan flair, while the Makarska region of-fers fine shingle and sand beaches. Active travellers will find hiking and mountain bike trails both in the Biokovo mountains and on the islands, and the crystal-clear waters are a paradise for divers and wind-surfers. Holidaymakers looking to party the night away should check out the styl-ish island of Hvar. The quieter island of Vis is still relatively off the beaten track (see the second Discovery Tour, p. 103).

BRAČ

(140–141 C–D4) *(∭ H–J 5–6)* **La dolce vita on idyllic beaches meets traditional agriculture in the hinterland: the island of Brač shows visitors two very different sides.**

Brač's most famous beach ★ *Zlatni rat*, or the "Golden Cape" is a strip of fine shingle that sometimes points to the east, sometimes to the west, depending on the currents of the sea. However, it would be

Photo: The beach of Zlatni rat, the "Golden Cape", on the island of Brač

City flair and bathing fun: lively ports, cosy konobas and remote beach coves

a shame to focus exclusively on this idyllic spit and ignore the rest of what is the largest island in Central Dalmatia (395 km²/152 mi², approx. 15,000 inhabitants). Bare, macchia-covered surfaces are as much a part of the landscape here as the irrigated and cultivated valley slopes planted with olive and fig trees or vines. Brač is blessed with a precious building material – namely its brilliant white limestone, which is known as "Brač marble" and was quarried as early as in Roman times. It possesses two major advantages: it is relatively soft, which means it is easy to "harvest" as the people of Brač say, and it is equally easy to work. It also hardens and becomes stronger over time. The stone is still excavated today in several of the island's quarries.

PLACES ON BRAČ

BOL AND THE SOUTH COAST
(141 D4) (*ØØ H6*)

The village of *Bol* (pop. 1,600) is spread out along the south coast at the foot of

The 16th-century Blaca hermitage is a popular destination for hikers

the island's highest mountain, *Vidova gora* (778 m/2,552 ft). Bol's popularity as a seaside resort is due to the several hundred-metre long fine shingle beach *Zlatni rat (Golden Cape)* and the village's mild climate, as the mountain shelters it from the cold north-easterly Bora wind. However in the middle of summer, you can feel like in a tin of sardines at this beautiful spot.

The picturesque centre of Bol is a maze of small streets clustered around the harbour, and lined with traditional stone houses. The village has a whole host of guesthouses, souvenir shops and restaurants, but there is also a niche for modern art: the *Galerija Dešković (June–Sept Tue–Sun 9am–noon, 6–11pm, Oct–May Tue–Sat 9am–3pm | 15 kuna)* exhibits works by contemporary Croatian creatives in a Baroque palace by the harbour. A short walk to the east will bring you to the *Dominican monastery (June–Oct daily 10am–noon, 4–7pm | 15 kuna | Anđelka Rabadana 4)*, whose muse-

um displays prehistoric artefacts and a painting by Tintoretto, among other items. The monastery's gardens and the nearby ● shingle beach at **INSIDER TIP** *Martinšćica* are also well worth a visit.

The reliably consistent Maestral wind makes Bol one of Dalmatia's windsurfing centres (alongside Orebić). You can also hire mountain bikes and kayaks from *Big Blue Sport (Podan Glavice 2 | www.bigbluesport.com)* on Borak beach. An old mill forms the centrepiece of the comfortable *Konoba Mlin (Ante Starčevića 11 | tel. 021 63 53 76 | Moderate)*, where we recommend that you order the *pašticada.* Slightly higher up the hill above all the hustle and bustle lies the restaurant *Ranč (Hrvatskih domobrana 6 | tel. 021 63 56 35 | Budget–Moderate)*, which mainly serves rustic grilled dishes and traditional Dalmatian cuisine. In the evening, partygoers congregate in the bar *Varadero (Frane Radića 1)*. Inside the **INSIDER TIP** Dominican monastery, there is a hotel with modern furnishings and an exceptionally romantic ambience, located just a few steps from the beach *(29 rooms | Expensive | book via Santo Agency | Frane Radića 16 | tel. 091 7 81 89 99 | www.santo-bol-croatia.com)*. Among the beach hotels located to the west of the village, the *Bluesun Elaphusa (307 rooms | Put Zlatnog rata 46 | tel. 01 3 84 42 88 | www.hotelelaphusabrac. com | Expensive)* indulges its guests with a generous wellness centre.

A boat excursion takes visitors from Bol to the "desert" *(pustinja):* to *Blaca hermitage (Pustinja Blaca)*, founded by monks in the 16th century after fleeing the Ottomans at the remote head of a gorge *(45 min. walk from the docking point | 120 kuna)*. The monks here still use the old-Croatian *glagolica* ecclesiastical alphabet, and there is a small *museum (Tue–Sun 9am–5pm | 40 kuna)*.

There is another hermitage 6 km/3.7 miles to the west of Bol in *Murvica*, where hermits lived in the *Dragon's Cave (Zmajeva špilja)* from the 15th century onwards. The name comes from the dragon reliefs carved into the cave walls by early Christians (register your visit in advance at the tourist info in Bol).
Information: *Tourist Info (Porat Bolskih pomoraca | Bol | tel. 021 63 56 38 | www. bol.hr)*

VILLAGES IN THE ISLAND'S INTERIOR
(140–141 C–D4) *(M H5–6)*

The houses in the shepherd village of *Gornji Humac* 10 km/6.2 miles to the north of Bol are built out of undressed stone, with roofs made of stone slabs due to the powerful winds up on the plateau (485 m/1,590 ft). The rustic ● *Konoba Tomić (tel. 021 64 72 28 | Budget)* also rents out accomodation *(9 rooms)* while the restaurant serves organically grown meat and vegetables.

The village of *Škrip* 20 km/12.5 miles further north-west is the oldest settlement on the island, and is believed to have been inhabited since 1,400 BC. The centre of the village is wonderfully preserved and boasts defensive walls, a church and a tower. The *Muzej otoka Brača (daily in*

⭐ **Zlatni rat**
The "Golden Cape" is Brač's paradise beach → p. 52

⭐ **Hvar Town**
A perfect collection of historic buildings with an added dose of liveliness → p. 58

⭐ **Makarska Riviera**
15 holiday villages scattered along the most beautiful beaches in Central Dalmatia → p. 61

⭐ **Diocletian's Palace**
A city forming a palace, or vice versa? Split blends ancient and modern → p. 66

⭐ **Sv. Duje Cathedral**
This Christian church hides a pagan secret: the Emperor's mausoleum → p. 67

⭐ **Trogir**
The whole city is a work of art from Gothic to Baroque, inspired by a laid-back Mediterranean lifestyle → p. 70

⭐ **Blue Grotto (Modra špilja)**
The waters here on the island of Biševo glow with a fairy-tale blue – but only at lunchtime, between 11am and noon → p. 73

MARCO POLO HIGHLIGHTS

summer 8am–8pm | 12 kuna) in the 16th-century *Radojković Tower* explains the history of the village, and reminders of Roman times are provided by a relief of Hercules, as well as a mausoleum.

Brač's white stone has also been a source of inspiration to artists, and a regular clan of sculptors lives and works in *Donji Humac* (3 km/1.9 miles east of Škrip, 20 km/12.5 miles northwest of Bol). Great-grandfather Jakšić opened the workshop in 1903, and the youngest Jakšić is the sculptor Lovre junior, whose works transform stone into a seemingly fluid material. The family is happy to welcome visitors to their ● **INSIDERTIP** *Galerija Jakšić (no fixed opening times | tel. 021 64 77 10 | www.drazen-jaksic.hr)*.

PUČIŠĆA (141 D4) (*∅ H5*)

It is easy to see that this town (pop. 1,700), situated in a deep and narrow cove on the island's north coast, is a centre for Brač's characteristic stone. With its bright houses arranged around the harbour, its souvenir stands selling bowls and figurines carved from white limestone, and its attractive *Renaissance Church of the Assumption* with tombs carved by stonemasons from the island, Pučišća gives a thoroughly authentic impression.

There are plenty of small shingle beaches to visit, as well as the glorious **INSIDERTIP** *Uvala Luke* around 3 km/1.9 mile to the east. Here, five coves nestle against an inlet of the sea, and in Luke cove the *Taverna Pipo (tel. 021 7 84 54 95 | www.pipo1.com | Expensive)* serves freshly caught fish. In Pučišća itself, the bistro *Fontana (Trg B. Deskovića 4 | tel. 021 63 35 15 | Moderate)* with its simple dishes is worth a visit. The *Pansion Lučica (10 rooms | Ivana Pavla II 1 | tel. 021 63 32 62 | www.pansion-lucica.com | Budget)* offers accommodation a short distance away from the cove, in a setting surrounded by Mediterranean greenery.

SUPETAR (140 C4) (*∅ H5*)

The town (pop. 3,200) of St Peter (Sv. Petar) on the north coast is Brač's second-largest holiday destination as well as an arrival point for car ferries from the mainland. The old town is dominated by the *Church of St Mary Annunciation* with its impressive Baroque staircase. A 15-minute walk along the beach will take you to the picturesque cemetery at the tip of the Sv. Nikola peninsula. The shingle and sand beaches to the west of the landspit Bili rat offer an alternative to the crowded main beach; here, you can find coves lined with shady pine forests. The majority of the large beach hotels gather around the Vela Luka bay to the west. Further afield, you will also find nice (sun)bathing spots in the smaller and larger bays.

At the *Konoba Luš (daily from 5pm | Put Viščica 55 | tel. 099 8 03 36 46 | Moderate)* you can dine in the attractive setting of an olive grove, while the *Velaris Tourist Resort (86 rooms, 6 apts. | Put Vele Luke 10 | tel. 021 60 66 06 | www.velaris.hr | Moderate–Expensive)* offers contemporary design and interiors with a modern main building and a historic villa. For more individual lodgings try the family-owned *Villa Adriatica (24 rooms | Put Vele Luke 31 | tel. 021 75 50 10 | www.villaadriatica.com | Moderate–Expensive)* decorated in warm colours, this establishment also boasts a good restaurant.

You can reach many other beaches and attractive villages by bike; visit *Freni Opačak (Vlačica bb | tel. 095 5 21 76 11 | www.rent-a-bike-brac.com)* for well-maintained bicycles and trip advice.

A few kilometres to the east you will find the peaceful village of *Splitska,* set idyllically on the slopes of a deep cove. The picturesque village of *Mirca,* 4 km/2.5

Owners anchor their boats in Supetar's port while they go off to enjoy the nightlife

miles to the west, is also worth a visit. At the *Muzej uljarstva (tel. 021 63 09 00)* you can learn how olive oil is pressed (advance booking required, oils can also be purchased).
Information: *Tourist Info (Porat 1 | Supetar | tel. 021 63 09 00 | www.supetar.hr)*

The connections *Split–Supetar* as well as *Jelsa (on Hvar)* and *Bol* run several times a day *(www.jadrolinija.hr)*.

HVAR

(140–141 C–E 4–5) *(H–J6)* **The Croatian Ibiza is a hot-spot, but away from the celebrities flocking to the island's capital Hvar you can still find down-to-earth Konobas and unspoilt beach coves.**
Hvar (pop. 11,000) measures just under 300 km²/116 mi² and is Croatia's most cosmopolitan island loved by VIPS. In Summer, the purple lavender blossoms cast clouds of fragrance over the island. The most beautiful beaches are found on the neighbouring *Pakleni otoci,* the "hell islands", which can be reached by taxi boat (approx. 40 kuna/person). The name doesn't really fit this bathing and snorkelling paradise. But it's not *pakleni* (hell), but *paklina* (tar pitch, used to aterproof ships) the islands are named after. On a INSIDER TIP guided kayak tour with *Hvar Adventure (Jurja Matijevića 20 | 4 hrs incl. snack and wine 375 kuna | tel. 021 71 78 13 | www.hvar-adventure.com)* participants paddle from cove to cove while the sun sets in the background. It is advisable to hire an electric bike in order to explore the mountainous island of Hvar on two wheels. Well-maintained bikes can be rented from *e-bike croatia (bike from 180 kuna/day | Ive Roic 6 | tel. 091 5 84 98 41 | www.e-bike-croatia.com)* in Hvar.

PLACES ON HVAR

HVAR TOWN ★ (140 C4) (*Ⅲ H6*)

During the summer, an armada of luxury yachts bob at their moorings along the shoreline promenade, the Riva, while their wealthy owners party in the clubs and restaurants of the town (pop. 4,200). Hvar attempts to shake off its party image by implementing draconian measures for example to those caught sightseeing in beachwear.

Fortunately, most of these VIPs pay little attention to Hvar's real attractions, so you can still take a relaxed stroll through the old town. The *Trg Sv. Stjepana* leading from the harbour *(mandrač)* to the *Sv. Stjepan* cathedral is a feast for the eyes, and this main square, or *Pjaca*, as residents call it, is rounded off by the cathedral's Renaissance facade and elegantly structured tower. Another striking building is the 16th-century *Arsenal,* which was used to conceal Venetian warships from prying eyes and to store grain.

In the formerly aristocratic quarter of *Groda* – which runs from the *Pjaca* almost all the way up the hill to the fortress – you can find the *Baroque Benedictine Convent Samostan Benediktinki (June–Sept Mon–Fri 10am–noon, 5–7pm | 10 kuna),* where the nuns make filigree doilies from agave fibres. The most beautiful examples of their work are on display in the small museum. From the ● ⬈ *Španjola fortress (summer, daily 8am–midnight; spring/autumn 9am–9pm | 40 kuna)* you can look out over the old town and the neighbouring archipelago of the *Pakleni otoci,* and explore an exhibition of archaeological artefacts.

Peace and quiet can be found at the *Franciscan convent Franjevački samostan (Mon–Sat 9am–3pm, 5–7pm | 35 kuna | Put križa),* situated to the south of the centre. This 15th century convent contains a *museum* displaying discoveries from below the sea, as well as a stunning cloister. You won't want to leave the neighbouring garden with its 300-year-old cypresses.

Hrvoje Tomičić offers sophisticated cuisine at **INSIDER TIP** *Kod Kapetana (Fabrika 30 | tel. 021 74 22 30 | Expensive)*: everything here is freshly prepared, from lobster to lamb, all with a view of the old town. Away from the hustle and bustle and close to the Franciscan convent, Đorđota Vartal of the *Restoran Vartal (Fulgencija Careva 1 | tel. 021 74 30 77 | restoran-vartal.com | Moderate)* specialises in meat dishes.

Evenings in Hvar typically begin with a *korzo* – an evening stroll on the main square. The stylish *Carpe Diem* on the promenade is a popular place to have a drink, but for a more relaxed atmosphere visit the bar *Zimmer Frei (Gornja cesta)* in a back street in the old town. A little further on you will find the hotspot *Ka' Lavanda Music Bar (Mate Miličića 7 | www.kalavanda.com)*. The *Lola Bar (Sveti Marak 8 | Moderate)* serves delicious cocktails and burgers alongside great music – try the RunLolaRun cocktail! *Carpe Diem* offers a private shuttle service to its *Carpe Diem Beach (May–Sept daily 8am–8pm, longer at events | www.carpe-diem-hvar. com)* in *Stipanska bay* on the island of *Marinkovac,* where sun worshippers will find entertainment in the form of a restaurant, lounge bar and DJ sets.

The seafront promenade and harbour are lined with several luxury hotels. The *Palace (73 rooms | Trg Sv. Stjepana 5 | tel. 021 75 04 00 | www.suncanihvar.com | Expensive)* offers historic flair and an incomparable breakfast terrace. The simpler hotel *Croatia (22 rooms | Majerovica bb | tel. 021 74 24 00 | www.hotelcroatia. net | Moderate)* is hidden away slightly to the west, with views of the Pakleni otoci archipelago. The ● 🌏 guesthouse *Tonči* *(6 rooms | tel. 021 74 12 44 | www.pe nsion-tonci.com/index_en.htm | Budget– Moderate)* on the island of *Sv. Klement* places an emphasis on sustainability; its Konoba serves homegrown organic vegetables.

an attitude. This settlement was originally founded in the 4th century BC by Greek colonists and lies on a deep and narrow cove in the north of the island. Stari Grad was once an important cultural centre: the Croatian Renaissance poet Petar Hektorović (1487–1572) hosted the

The main square, Pjaca, in Hvar resembles a VIP lounge in summer

Accessible cycling destinations include the village of *Brusje,* a lavender farming centre situated 6 km/3.7 miles to the north-east of Hvar. Lavender products are sold almost everywhere here, including aromatic lavender honey. For organic food products such as olive oil, cheese or wine, visit the 🌏 *Green House Hvar* *(Kroz Burak 27)*.

Information: *Tourist Info (Trg Sv. Stjepana | tel. 021 74 29 77 | www.tzhvar.hr)r*

STARI GRAD (141 D4) (*∅ H6*)

Hvar's counterpoint is the town of Stari Grad (pop. 2,400), which welcomes visitors with a relaxed Mediterrane-

brightest minds of his time for discussions at his fortress-like *Villa Tvrdalj (May– Oct daily 10am–1pm, 5:30–8:30pm | 15 kuna)* The grounds include a fishpond set in an arcade courtyard, whose walls are decorated with Latin aphorisms that offer an insight into the poet's philosophical world. Hektorović and his daughter Lucrezia are also depicted in a portrait in the church of the *Dominican monastery,* which was painted by none other than Tintoretto. You can also inspect the remains of the ancient city walls close to the *Sv. Ivan church.*

The *Stari Grad Plain* – a fertile karst valley running from Stari Grad to Jelsa – is a Unesco World Heritage Site, as its wine and olive plantations are still arranged in the pattern set out by Greek colonists in the 4th century BC. The stone walls bordering these fields and the huts used by the farmers are also based on ancient designs. A top dinner recommendation is the **INSIDER TIP** *Konoba Zvijezda mora (Trg Petra Zoranića | tel. 099 2 99 16 03 | www.zvijezdamora.com | Expensive)*, where the head chef Tomislav Subašić cooks regional products and herbs to perfection. In the village of *Dol* 4 km/2.5 miles to the east, the ● *Konoba Kokot (from 6pm | Kuničića dvor 8 | Dol St Ana | tel. 091 5 11 42 88 | Budget)* serves regional cuisine with organically sourced ingredients, and you can find goat's cheese of all kinds as well as kid meat on the menu. **INSIDER TIP** *Hidden House (Duolnjo Kola 13 | www.hidden-house.com | Expensive)* run by the British couple Amanda and Chris, is an insider accommodation tip. You need to book early because this lovingly and stylishly furnished Bed and Breakfast only has four rooms. Information: *Tourist Info (Obala Franje Tuđmana 1 | tel. 021 76 57 63 | www.stari-grad-faros.hr)*

VRBOSKA, JELSA AND SURROUNDINGS (141 D4) *(∅ H6)*

The two harbour towns of *Vrboska* and *Jelsa* are located on the island's northern coast to the east of Stari Grad, and are notable for their unique settings on deep, sheltered coves. Vrboska's relaxed atmosphere and the shingle coves on the *Glavica* peninsula attract plenty of day-trippers during the summer. Aside from the narrow harbour with its ancient stone bridge, the town's main sight is its 16th-century fortified church of *Sv. Marija (daily in summer 10am–noon, 7:30–9pm | 15 kuna),* which sits on a hill above the town. *Jelsa* has a much more touristy feel. Here you can find a number of campsites, including **INSIDER TIP** *Camp Grebišće (tel.*

Towering over the Makarska Riviera is the Biokovo peak Sveti Jure

021 76 11 91 | www.grebisce.hr | Budget) 2 km/1.2 mile to the south of the town, which boasts beautifully arranged terraces overlooking an idyllic cove. Visit the *Konoba Dvor Duboković (from 6pm | tel. 098 172 17 26 | dvordubokovic.hr | Moderate)* in the village of Pitve 2 km/1.2 mile away for hearty Dalmatian fare served in a rustic ambience. We recommend sampling the homemade sour cherry and rose liqueurs! Travellers with an interest in wine cultivation should make the trip from Pitve to Zavala (approx. 5 km/3.1 miles) and continue a further 7 km/4.3 miles along the coast towards the west until they reach *Sv. Nedjelja*. Here, you can judge the effects of the special climate and soil for yourself in the *Konoba Bilo Idro (tel. 021 74 57 09 | Expensive)*. The vintner Zlatan Plenković presses the best wines on the island, including the famous *Zlatan otok*. You can also dine on fresh fish, or a platter of *pršut* and cheese.

7 km/4.3miles to the east of Jelsa is the ethnic village *Humac (free admission)*, a former herding village with stone houses from the 17th century which has been carefully restored. You can even spend the night in one of the rooms. Another appealing option is the traditional *Konoba Humac (tel. 091 5 23 94 63 | reservation advisable | www.facebook.com/ Konoba-Humac-357534557644483 | Moderate)* which offers tours to the *Caves of Grapčevo* to the south.

Information: *Tourist Info Vrboska (tel. 021 77 41 37 | www.vrboska.info)*; *Tourist Info Jelsa (tel. 021 76 10 17 | www.tzjelsa.hr)*

BOAT CONNECTIONS

Several ferries a day between *Split–Stari Grad/Hvar* and between *Drvenik–Sućuraj/ Hvar,* and there is a bi-weekly service during the peak season *Ancona (Italy)–Stari Grad/ Hvar (www.jadrolinija.hr)*.

MAKARSKA RIVIERA

(141 D–E4) *(ꞎ J 5–6)* The coastal road along the flanks of the Biokovo mountains winds tightly around coves and fjords, running past tiny fishing villages, fragrant macchia, vineyards, and the palm-lined promenades of bathing resorts.

The mountain range is what gives the ★ *Makarska Riviera* its mild climate, acting as a shield against the icy gusts of the Bora, while the islands of Brač, Hvar and Korčula protect the coast from the waves of the sea. With such a high degree of natural protection, it was inevitable that the Riviera would become a holiday destination. Alongside modern hotel complexes there are plenty of campsites.

PLACES ON THE MAKARSKA RIVIERA

BIOKOVO MOUNTAINS (141 E4) *(ꞎ J5–6)* This steep, dry karst landscape, part of the Dinaric Alps, is a protected Nature Park *(admission 50 kuna | www.biokovo. com)*, but seems almost devoid of vegetation at first glance. However, closer inspection reveals a surprising variety of flora, including countless endemic species which you can also see at the *Botanical Garden* in Kotišina (located above the village, free of charge). Hiking trails pass through thick beech and pine forests, skirting sinkholes and caves, old stone churches and the remnants of fortifications. The highest mountain in the Biokovo is *Sv. Jure* (1,762 m/5,780 ft), and a narrow, exposed road leads up to the summit. The peak can be scaled in around two hours from the *Dom Vošac* hut – a 450 m/1,475 ft ascent.

The more authentic side of Makarska away from the crowds of tourists and beach entertainment

BLUE AND RED LAKES (141 E3) (*M J5*)

It's well worth leaving the beach for a day to take a bathing trip into the Dalmatian hinterland (approx. 35 km/22 miles from Makarska) to the *Blue Lake (Modro jezero),* north of Imotski. Although you can't always swim in the karst lake (it can dry up in summer), you may catch the locals playing a game of football on the lake bed. It's impressive whatever time of year you visit: the lake lies in a 900 m/3000 ft deep sinkhole. A paved footpath leads down to the bottom.

Its neighbour, the *Red Lake (Crveno jezero),* is in fact not really red. It was given its name by the red cliffs which surround the circumference of the lake. *From the Blue Lake, drive along the road heading south for approx. 1 km/0.6 mile westwards*

MAKARSKA (141 E4) (*M J6*)

Like most of the older settlements along the Riviera, Makarska (pop. 13,500) is made up of an upper section spread along the side of the mountain and a lower town. Both have now grown together into a single holiday resort, centred on the lively shoreline promenade and its extension. The historic centre extends around the *Trg F. A. Kačića,* where the bell tower of the *Sv. Marko* church (18th century) rises decoratively in front of the rocky backdrop of the Biokovo mountains. A few Baroque *Palazzi* are preserved, including those built by the Ivanišević family *(Trg F. A. Kačića)* and the Tonoli family *(Obala kralja Tomislava 16).* The Franciscan monastery is home to the *Malakološki muzej (Mon–Sat 10am–noon, 5–7pm, Sun 10am–noon | 15 kuna | Franjevački put 1)* with its rich collection of snails and shellfish. The INSIDER TIP *Imagine Art* gallery *(Kalalarga 1)* beckons a few metres away where artist Marijeta Lozina exhibits her own impressions of sea life.

Makarska's 2 km/1.2 mile-long sand/shingle beach runs around the bay to the north of the centre. There is a comprehensive range of sporting activities such as parasailing, windsurfing and diving – see for instance *Parasailing Makarska (Put Cvitačke 2a | tel. 098 9 63 19 18)* or the diving centre *More Sub (K.P. Krešimira 43 | tel. 021 611 7 27 | www.more-sub-makarska.hr)*.

Countless restaurants and taverns compete for customers, offering Dalmatian cuisine and terraces with sea views. *Ivo (Ante Starčevića 41 | tel. 021 611 2 57 | Budget–Moderate)* is located in town away from the waterfront; but what it lacks in views it more than makes up for with its culinary offering. If you don't want to forgo the sight of the waves then try *DiVino (Šetalište F. Tuđmana | tel. 099 4 10 21 53 | Expensive)* – an ultra-stylish restaurant with prices that are very reasonable considering its quality and location. The *Wine Bar Grabovac (Trg F.A. Kačića | tel. 098 9 34 12 26)* is a popular place to stop for an early-evening aperitif or a small snack before guests move on elsewhere. *Marineta (daily 9am–2am | Marineta 7 | tel. 021 616 8 86)* is popular among night owls. Alongside the usual package hotels *(www.hoteli-makarska. hr | Moderate–Expensive)* you can stay at *Porin (8 rooms | Marineta 2 | tel. 021 613 7 44 | www.hotel-porin.hr | Moderate)* overlooking the harbour.

Information: *Tourist Info (Obala kralja Tomislava 16 | Tel. 021 612 0 02 | www.makarska-info.hr)*

NORTH OF MAKARSKA
(141 D–E4) (*ɷ J5–6*)

INSIDER TIP *Bratuš* lies just under 10 km/6 miles to the north, and to visit its old stone houses and its small cove is almost to travel back in time. The *Villa Babin Ranč (7 rooms, 6 apts. | tel. 021 62 13 33 | www.makarska-bratus.com | Budget)* lies in peaceful surroundings, with idyllic shingle coves just a few steps away. The *Konoba Bratuš (Bratuš 46 | tel.*

021 54 85 48 | Budget) directly on the waterfront offers friendly service and fine cuisine.

The skyline of the holiday resort *Baška Voda* is dominated by the imposing Biokovo mountains. A wide selection of bars and restaurants can be found together on the shingle beach. In *Palac (Obala Sv. Nikole 2 | tel. 021 62 05 44 | Moderate)* you can sit under shady trees and tuck into fresh seafood.

Nearby *Brela* provides shingle beaches, gastronomic offerings and sporting activities for unbridled holiday fun. The rocky island of *Kamen Brela* with its thick covering of pine trees is popular among photographers, and lies off the main beach of *Dugi rat.* Formerly known by the name *Punta rata,* this sand/shingle beach is often very busy in the summer. Accommodation by **INSIDER TIP** *Abuela's Beach House (4 flats | Jardula 20 | tel. 021 61 90 03 | www.abuelasbeachhouse.*

com | Moderate): colourfully decorated holiday flats with a dose of Latin flair, their owners being South Americans with Croatian roots.

Information: *Tourist Info (Trg Alojzija Stepin-ca | tel. 021 618 455 | www.brela. hr)*

SOUTH OF MAKARSKA (141 E4) (*Ⓜ J6*)

Tučepi is directly connected to Makarska and differs little from the Riviera's main town. Here you can find *Nugal Beach,* a famous nudist beach shielded from prying eyes by steep rocky cliffs. Head uphill for 45 minutes to reach *Gornji Tučepi,* where you will find a gourmet's paradise surrounded by glorious views: the ☆ *Restaurant Jeny (Gornji Tučepi 33 | tel. 091 5 87 80 78 | www.restaurant-jeny.hr | Expensive)* which serves fine modern interpretations of Dalmatian cuisine.

Živogošće is shielded from winds blowing from the country's interior by the 1,155 m/3,789 ft *Sutvid;* here, the mountains come so close to the shore that idyllic beaches such as *Mala Duba* practically nestle against the rock face. Accommodation is available in private rooms.

Information: *Tourist Info (Kraj 103 | Tučepi | tel. 021 62 31 00 | tucepi.com)*

OMIŠ

(141 D3) (*Ⓜ H5*) This former pirates' lair (pop. 16,000) spreads out on both sides of the Cetina river, which carves a path through the Dinaric Alps and emerges here at the head of a gorge.

Slavic pirates used this sheltered location as a base from the 11th until the 15th centuries, and only in 1444 did Venice manage to conquer Omiš. Two fortresses high up on the cliff watch over the old town's quiet streets, which are lined with stone houses.

FOOD & DRINK

KONOBA MILO

Among the many restaurants here, Milo stands out with its personal service and delicious Dalmatian cuisine. *Knezova Kačića 15 | tel. 021 86 11 85 | Moderate*

SPORTS & ACTIVITIES

Omiš boasts beautiful shingle and even sandy beaches on both sides of the Cetina, including the shallow waters of *Velika plaža,* where parasailing and beach volleyball are popular. For a dose of adrenalin try the zipline, where you hang from a cable 150 m/492 ft up and shoot across the canyon at speeds of up to 65 km/h/40 mph. *Agencija Malik (approx. 400 kuna | Josipa Pupačića 4 | tel. 095 8 22 22 21 | zipline-croatia.com).*

ENTERTAINMENT

BAR LIX

This colourfully decorated bar is one of the most popular hangouts in Omiš. *Daily with open end | Knezova Kačića*

WHERE TO STAY

VILLA DVOR ☆

Guests of this on the slope opposite the old town njoy an impressive panorama. *23 rooms | Mosorska cesta 13 | tel. 021 86 34 44 | www.hotel-villadvor.hr | Moderate*

INFORMATION

TOURIST INFO

Trg Kneza Miroslava | tel. 021 86 13 50 | www.tz-omis.hr

Omiš - a former pirates' lair is now a popular hiking destination for tourists

WHERE TO GO

CETINA GORGE (141 D3) (*🗺 H5*)
This forested valley is an attractive destination for hikers and cyclists, and rafting and canoe trips through the gorge from *Penšići* are also popular. After 2 hours, your dinghy will arrive at the restaurant *Radmanove mlinice (tel. 021 86 20 73 | www.rad manove-mlinice.hr | Moderate)*, where you get cold beer and lamb cooked in a *peka*. Rafting excursions are available from e.g.*Kentona (approx. 230 kuna| Drage Ivaniševića 15 | www.rafting-cetina.com)*.

SPLIT

⚏⚏ MAP INSIDE THE BACK COVER
(140 C3) (*🗺 H5*) **In the foreground, there's the bustling harbour. Residents and tourists stroll along the Riva in front of the walls of Diocletian's palace, admiring its floral decorations. Dalmatia's biggest city and most important ferry port offers visitors an attractive vista.**
The centre of *Split* (180,000 inhabitants) is shut off from all traffic, noise and crowds: behind the mighty walls of the Roman imperial palace you will hear nothing but the cooing of pigeons and the church bells. The huge palace district (215 x 180 m/705 x 590 ft) was built around 240–312 for the Emperor Diocletian, a persecutor of Christians, and formed the basis for the city of Split: today, it harbours sections of the old town. Inhabitants of the Roman city of Salona sought refuge behind the palace's walls in the face of Slavic incursions during the 7th century, and the Roman buildings have withstood 1,500 years of habitation almost miraculously well. In 1979 the palace was designated a Unesco World Heritage Site.

> **CITY WHERE TO START?**
> The best starting point for a sightseeing tour is the waterfront promenade **Obala Hrvatskog narodnog preporoda**, or **Riva** for short, in front of Diocletian's Palace. There is also a car park here, but it is often full (there is an alternative on Vukovarska ulica). To the west of the palace is the old town around the lively **Narodni trg.**

CHAEOLOGICAL MUSEUM
(ARHEOLOŠKI MUZEJ)

If you are not planning to visit the Salona archaeological site then visit Croatia's oldest archaeological museum (founded in 1820). It documents the history of the Romans in Dalmatia with the help of mosaics and other artefacts. *June–Sept Mon–Sat 9am–2pm, 4–8pm, Oct–May Tue–Fri 9am–2pm, 4–8pm, Sat 9am–2pm | 30 kuna | Zrinsko-Frankopanska 25*

DIOCLETIAN'S PALACE ★

From the Riva, visitors enter this ancient complex through its basement, the Podrumi *(June–Sept daily 8:30am–9pm, Oct–May shorter; closed Sun afternoon | 42 kuna)*. The high ceiling is supported on brick arches and walls that divide the basement up into 50 rooms using exactly the same floor plan as the imperial apartments above it. From here, a staircase takes you up to the open air, where you will find a *peristyle* surrounded by arcades with Corin-thian columns. A further staircase leads to the *vestibule,* the only room still preserved today, which offers a good overview of the rest of the ancient structure. On the right, the emperor's mausoleum was converted into *Sv. Duje Cathedral,* which rises from the peristyle, while diagonally opposite stands the *baptistery*, a former *Temple of Jupiter.* The *cardo* and *decumanus* – the two main streets crossing at right angles to each other in any Roman town – are today known as the *Ulica Dioklecijanova* and the *Krešimirova*, and lead to the city gates of the *Porta Ferrea* (Iron Gate) in the west, the *Porta Argentea* (Silver Gate) in the east, and the northern main gate of the *Porta Aurea* (Golden Gate).

TEMPLE OF JUPITER/BAPTISTERY

The small 5th-century temple (in the palace to the west of the peristyle), which was converted into a Christian baptistery in the 7th century, is guarded by a stone sphinx. Its cruciform baptismal font is ornamented with old croatian reliefs. *In summer daily 8:30am–7:30pm | 10 kuna*

Where once the Romans paid homage to their Emperor – the Peristyle is still a location for big occasions

SV. DUJE CATHEDRAL ★

At the heart of the cathedral is the octagonal mausoleum of the Roman emperor Diocletian, whose ornamented Corinthian columns now frame one of Dalmatia's most beautiful altars: Juraj Dalmatinac created the touching relief of the Flagellation of Christ in 1422. Also worthy of note are the richly decorated Roman portal and the treasury containing the relics of St Domnius *(15 kuna)*. Travellers with a head for heights should climb the 60 m/197 ft *bell tower* to enjoy the glorious views. *Mon–Sat 8:30am–7pm, Sun 12:30–6:30pm | joint ticket bell tower, treasury and baptistery 45 kuna*

MARJAN HILL

Split's green lung starts to the west of the harbour: the 3.5 km² peninsula of Marjan is covered in thick and shady greenery, and residents of Split come here to jog, cycle or swim. Nestled among the trees you will find chapels and churches dating from the 16th and 17th centuries, while a 378-step staircase built in 1924 takes you to the highest point (m/584 ft). After a stroll, take a brea in the *Café Vidilica (Nazorov prilaz 1)*. The peninsula is also fringed with shingle beaches such as *Bene, Ježinac* and *Kašjuni*.

Ivan Meštrović (1883–1962) is Croatia's most renowned sculptor and is mainly known for his monumental sculptures. In his summer residence, the ● *Galerija Meštrović*, shows the diversity and intricacy of his works. *May–Sept Tue–Sun 9am–7pm, therwise Tue–Sat 9am–4pm, Sun 10am–3pm | 40 kuna | Šetalište Ivana Meštrovića 46 | www.mestrovic.hr*

FOOD & DRINK

BUFFET FIFE

This harbour bar is simple and jolly; the food is tasty home-cooked fare that comes in huge portions. Among the people of Split the deep-fried little fish are an insider tip. *Trumbićeva obala 11 | tel. 021 34 52 23 | Budget*

LUKA

It's definitely worth queuing for what is by far the best ice cream in the city. Homemade ice cream in a variety of exotic flavours all made from natural ingredients. *Svačićeva 2 | de-de.facebook.com/ LukaIceCream*

KONOBA MATEJUŠKA

This tiny restaurant operates on a reservation-only basis and serves by far the best traditional cuisine, with plenty of fish. *Tomića Stine 3 | tel. 021 32 10 86 | www.villamatejuska.hr | Expensive*

VEGGIE OPTIONS

Tasty alternatives for vegetarians and vegans are available in the creative dishes at *Makrovega (Leština 2 | www.makrovega.hr | tel. 021 39 44 40 | Moderate)*,

bines traditional recipes with contemporary trends. *Ulica Marka Marulića | tel. 021 35 51 35 | zinfandelfoodandwinebar. com | Moderate*

SHOPPING

STARI PAZAR MARKET
A fruit and vegetable market next to Diocletian's Palace. Also sells souvenirs. *Daily*

FASHION
Creations from Croatian fashion designers hang from the clothes racks at the *Think Pink (Zadarska 8 and Marulićeva 1)*. boutique. The friendly store ❤ *Krug (Nepotova 1 | www.krugstore.com)*. in the old town specialises in natural chic clothing made from sustainable and fairtrade materials. The *ID Concept Store (Bana Jelačića 3)* offers an eclectic mix of romantic clothing from Croatian and international designers.

PODRUMI ●
Parts of the subterranean vaults of Diocletian's Palace are devoted to market stands selling souvenirs, books, handmade jewellery and beautiful replicas of Roman mosaic motifs.

BEACHES

Split's city beach *Bačvice* (shingle/concrete) lies to the south-east of the old town. Residents come here not just to bathe, but also to play the popular sport of **INSIDER TIP** *picigin*, a kind of volleyball played in shallow water. Additional beaches can be found on the Marjan peninsula and in the coves to the south, such as the popular *Obojena svjetlost* in *Kaštelet*.

A shopping stroll in the Palace cellar

as cheap snacks in *Vege Fast Food (Put Porta 2 | Budget)* or in the sophisticated ❤ *Up Café (Domovinskog rata 29a | www. upcafe.hr | Moderate)*.

INSIDER TIP ZINFANDEL FOOD & WINE BAR
This cosy venue with bags of atmosphere is well known for its creativity and com-

ENTERTAINMENT

In this young city of students, there are a lot of clubs and bars to choose from. Start your evening with a relaxed aperitif at the ✹ *Café Vidilica (Nazorov prilaz 1)* with a distant view of the Adriatic islands, or at *Getto (Dosud 10)*, where guests can sink into recliner chairs amid flowers and water fountains. The combination of jazz and old books creates a special flair at the *Marvlvs Library Jazz Club (Papalićeva 4)*. Later in the evening, Split's hip young crowd congregate at *Vanilla (Poljudski put)*, at the exclusive Hemingway (*Mediteranskih igara 5*) or one of the clubs around Bačvice beach. If you visit in September, do take a look at the programme of the *Split Film Festival (www.splitfilmfestival.hr)*. Information at the tourist information office or at *www.hnk-split.hr*.

WHERE TO STAY

KAŠTEL ✹

This friendly B&B in the old town rents out rooms, apartments and a luxury suite, all of which have wonderful views of the Riva. *8 rooms, 2 apartments, 1 suite | Mihovilova širina 5 | tel. 021 34 39 12 | www.kastelsplit.com | Budget–Moderate*

PERISTIL

Modern design within ancient walls; the rooms may be a little dark, but it's worth staying here to enjoy a peaceful retreat at the heart of the city. *12 rooms | Poljana kraljice Jelene 5 | tel. 021 32 90 70 | www.hotelperistil.com| Moderate*

VILLA ANA

Friendly guesthouse in an old stone building, not far from the ferry terminal. *5 rooms | Vrh Lučac 16 | tel. 021 48 27 15 | www.villaana-split.hr | Budget–Moderate*

BOAT CONNECTIONS

Regular ferry or catamaran connections to *Brač, Hvar, Korčula, Lastovo, Vis* and *Šolta (www.jadrolinija.hr)*.

INFORMATION

TOURIST INFO

Peristil | tel. 021 34 56 06 | www.visitsplit.com

WHERE TO GO

KAŠTELA – ROUTE OF THE CASTLES
(140 C3) (*ω G–H5*)

The so-called "Route of the castles" connects seven castles that have evolved out of fortress-like complexes from the 15th/16th centuries, situated on the bay west of Split: *Sućurac, Gomilica, Kambelovac, Lukšić, Stari, Novi* and *Štafilić.*

Under Habsburg rule this section of the coast became the Split Riviera, as testified by its many historic villas and royal hotels (most of which are now rather dilapidated). Socialist Yugoslavia transformed it into a base for heavy industry, and as a result the modern Kaštela is something of a mish-mash, with dreamily beautiful parks and a few restored castles bordering alongside rusting industrial complexes. *Kaštel Gomilica* is worth a visit, perched majestically on a rocky island.

The biblical garden ● *Biblijski vrt (Put Gospe Stomorije bb | free admission)* in *Stomorija* offers a tranquil paradise between biblical sculptures and plants.
Information: *Tourist Info (Brce 1 | Kaštel Lukšić | Tel. 021 22 79 33 | kastela-info.hr)*

KLIS ✹ (140 C3) (*ω H5*)

This imposing fortress was long known as the "key to Dalmatia" and towers above the town of the same name, situated approx. 14 km/8.6 miles before you reach Split. Its strategic position meant that it was used by Roman, Croatian, Venetian, and Ottoman Emperors – and even by rulers with dragons: Klis is namely one of the filming locations for a "Game of Thrones". Although you won't see the approach of enemy troops from the watch towers today, you will be treated to amazing views over the coastal landscape. The railings around the towers are precariously low to say the least and definitely not suitable for small children. *Daily 9:30am–4pm | admission 40 kuna | tvrdavaklis.com*

ŠOLTA (140 C4) *(fff G5)*

This island (58 km², pop. 1,700) lies just off the coast by Split, and has a wonderfully rural feel despite its proximity to the city. Its olive groves produce one of the best oils in Croatia, and accommodation is available almost exclusively in private rooms and apartments. The island's tourist centres are *Nečujam* and *Stomorska* in the east, while the highly comfortable *Hotel Martinis Marchi (6 suites | Put Sv. Nikole 51 | tel. 021 718838 | www. martinis-marchi.com | Expensive)* in *Maslinica* in the west is situated in a historic castle. Bathing spots can be found in the coves along the northern coast; the rocky south coast is only accessible from the sea.

Information: *Tourist Info (Podkuća 8 | Grohote | tel. 021 654657 | www.visitsolta.com)*

TROGIR

MAP INSIDE THE BACK COVER

(140 B3) *(fff G5)* **No city in Dalmatia boasts such well-preserved Romanesque and Gothic architecture as ★ Trogir (pop. 13,000).**

The elongated island, running between the mainland and the much larger island of Čiovo, has a dense covering of churches, palaces and town houses lining narrow streets, and the city's facades and courtyards boast 13th-15th century architectural details such as mullioned windows, arcades and fountains. Trogir is no museum, however, as this Unesco World Heritage Site is brought to life by residents and holidaymakers. The old town is connected to the modern quarters in the north and south by two bridges.

SIGHTSEEING

BENEDICTINE CONVENT (SAMOSTAN SV. NIKOLE)

The small museum of the convent houses valuable paintings and church treasures, yet they all pale in front of a Greek stone relief from the 3rd century BC. It depicts Kairos, whom the Greeks revered as the god of the opportune moment. *Summer daily 10am–1pm, 4–5:45pm, should it be closed, just call: tel. 021 88 16 31 | 30 kuna | Gradska 2*

KAMERLENGO FORTRESS

Built in the 15th century, this fortress didn't just protect Trogir from attackers; it also sheltered the treasurers from the wrath of the townsfolk. *July–Sept daily 8am–9pm, May/June, Oct 10am–7pm | 25 kuna | in the west of the old town island*

MAIN SQUARE (TRG IVANA PAVLA II)

This square is located at the north-eastern end of the historic town. The elegant facade of the 15th-century *Ćipiko Palace* opposite *Sv. Lovro Cathedral* will impress visitors; its gothic triple-mullioned windows are designed by Andrija Aleši, while Nikola Firentinac was responsible for the enchanting inner courtyard. The eastern end of the square is dominated by the

Sightseeing made easy: all of Trogir's most splendid buildings are on its main square

13th-century *City Hall,* which was renovated during the Renaissance. If the inner courtyard is open then you will also be able to view its INSIDER TIP Romanesque staircase and a fountain.

SV. LOVRO CATHEDRAL

The harmonically integrated architectural styles of this church – from its Romanesque basement to the Renaissance forms of the upper floors of the tower – tell the story of its long construction, dating from the 13th to the 17th centuries. One masterpiece of the earliest Romanesque phase is the ● *main portal,* which was decorated by Master Radovan with a sequence of everyday scenes, while Adam and Eve stand on lions on the left and right-hand sides. Inside the church, the *side chapel* built by Andrija Aleši, Nikola Firentinac and Ivan Duknović for Bishop John of Trogir is of particular note – a bright and flawless Renaissance masterpiece. The 45 m/148 ft ⚲ *bell tower* offers a beautiful view over the old town. *In summer Mon–Sat 8am–8pm, Sun noon –6pm, otherwise Mon–Sat 9am–noon | 25 kuna*

FOOD & DRINK

ALKA

Charcoal-grilled fish and meat. What's special here, however, are the few tables on the intimate, romantic roof terrace. *Augustina Kažotića 15 | tel. 021 88 18 56 | www.restaurant-alka.hr | Expensive*

CALEBOTTA

Stylish bar-restaurant offering fresh Dalmatian cuisine at the heart of the old town, this place leaves nothing to be desired whether you go for breakfast, lunch or dinner. *Gradska 23 | tel. 021 79 64 13 | Moderate*

GROTA

The romantic cave restaurant "Grotto" in the neighbouring village of *Seget Donji* offers culinary underground delights and is a pilgrimage for couples planning a proposal. *Hrvatskih Žrtava 360 | tel. 021 62 64 98 | Moderate–Expensive*

WHERE TO STAY

PAŠIKE
Stylish rooms with antique furniture in a quiet street in the old town. *7 rooms, 1 apartment | Sinjska | tel. 021 88 51 85 | www.hotelpasike.com | Moderate*

INFORMATION

TOURIST INFO
Trg Ivana Pavla II/1 | tel. 021 88 56 28 | www.tztrogir.hr

WHERE TO GO

UNDERWATER STATIONS OF THE CROSS (140 B3) *(ⓜ G5)*
Religious tourism can be more adventurous than you may first think: The world's first underwater Stations of the Cross have been erected in Jelinak bay near Marina close to Trogir. The 14 stations depicting Jesus on the day of his crucifixion are replicated with 50 life-size sculptures. Beginner divers do not need to fear the 4 to 9 m/13 to 29 feet depths down to the biblical figures. A magical sight is when rays of sunlight fall onto the sculptures through the water's surface. Underwater lighting means you can go on a pilgrimage dive by night. Contact: diving club *Blue Nautica (Put Cumbrijana 19 | tel.099 6 60 02 69 | www.blue-nautica.com)*

VIS

(140 B5) *(ⓜ G6)* **The ferry trip from Split to the remote island of Vis (pop. 3,500) takes around two hours. Maybe the remoteness is why Vis is one of the few islands to remain relatively undiscovered by tourists, and is not short of idyllic coves and secluded beaches.**
The island was settled in the 4th century BC by ancient Greeks (who called it *Issa*),

Far out in the Adriatic lies Vis with the tranquil harbour town Komiža

followed by Romans and Slavs. Vis then came under Venetian rule during the 15th century. After the Venetians left, the Habsburgs took over for over a century, before Tito arrived in 1943 and set up a command centre. During the socialist era Vis became a naval base and access was restricted; only in 1992 did the 91 km² island open its doors to tourists. The former military building and underground tunnel of the "forbidden island" are rediscovered on the adventurous INSIDER TIP Military Tour *(bookable at the travel agency Vis Special | www.vis-special.com | 4-hour tour 410 kuna)*. Visitors will find fertile landscapes, a rugged coast dotted with idyllic coves, and the two small towns of *Komiža* and *Vis*. The second Discovery Tour (see p. 103) will help you explore the island on two wheels.

PLACES ON VIS

KOMIŽA (140 B5) (*Ø G6*)

Stone houses line the natural harbour, where fishermen used to weigh anchor to go in search of sardines. Today, this quiet town (pop. 1,200) is a popular destination for sailors. In the *Fishermen's Museum Ribarski muzej (daily 10am–noon, 8–11pm | 20 kuna)* in the Venetian ⚓ *watchtower* you can see a replica *falkuša* – a traditional fishing boat. Two shingle beaches, *Gusarica* and *Kamenica,* invite you to take a dip in the sea. Fish, lobster and seafood set the tone in the INSIDER TIP *Konoba Jastožera (Gundulićeva 6 | tel. 021 713 8 59 | Expensive)*.

VIS (140 B5) (*Ø G6*)

The island's main town (pop. 1,900) lies on a horseshoe-shaped cove on the north-eastern coast, and the traces of ancient Issa are already apparent from

the sea on your way into the harbour: on the tip of the spit there is a ● Greek *necropolis,* a little further down you will also find the foundations of a Roman bath (freely accessible). The *Archaeological Museum (June–Sept Mon–Fri 10am–1pm, 5–8pm, Sat 10am–1pm | 20 kuna | Šetalište viški boj 12)* in the former Habsburg harbour fort *(Baterija della Madonna)* displays beautiful amphorae, statues and everyday objects. Vis makes a good base for trips to the island; you can stay in the stylish hotel *San Giorgio (16 rooms | Petra Hectorovića 2 | tel. 021 60 76 30 | hotelsangiorgiovis.com | Moderate)*. The fact that the cosy *Konoba Kod Paveta (Ivana Farolfija 42 | tel. 021 711 3 44 | Moderate)* only boasts a small terrace is more than made up for by its delicious traditional dishes.

The experts at *ANMA Diving (Apolonia Zanelle 2 | tel. 091 5 21 39 44 | anma.hr)* will take you to the best diving spots. Information: *Tourist Info (Šetalište stare Isse 5 | tel. 021 71 70 17 | www.tz-vis.hr)*

BOAT CONNECTION

There is a car ferry between *Split–Vis* three times a day during the season.

WHERE TO GO

BIŠEVO (BLUE GROTTO) (140 B5) (*Ø G7*)

If you want to take a trip to this neighbouring island to see its famous ★ *Blue Grotto (Modra špilja)* you should enlist the help of an agency to take you from Komiža to the cave at the right time of day. Sunlight causes the water in the cave to glow with a radiant turquoise colour, but only for a short time around midday *(numerous agencies in Komiža, admission 70 kuna)*.

DUBROVNIK REGION

Dominated by the karst mountain scenery of the Dinaric Alps on the inland side, the most southern part of Dalmatia stretches along the border with Bosnia-Herzegovina and Montenegro to the sea as a long, narrow strip.

Everything in this region is oriented towards the water – from towns and parks to vineyards and villas. The mountainous ridges of the Pelješac peninsula and the islands of Korčula, Lastovo and Mljet rise from the sea alongside one another, running almost parallel to the coast.

This confined region gave rise to the city state of Ragusa, nowadays called Dubrovnik, which became a perpetual rival to Venice from the 13th century onwards. The city's old town with its impregnable walls is the undisputed high-light of any sightseeing tour of South Dalmatia; but there are also areas of natural beauty, such as the Elaphiti Islands or Mljet, and cultural treasures tucked away in places such as Korčula and Cavtat.

CAVTAT

(143 E6) (*M8*) **This small town (pop. 2,100) is nestled inside a deep cove surrounded by peninsulas. Its attractive forested coastline is lined with shingle beaches, while three beach hotels offer a chance to relax and indulge in sporting activities.**

A Roman settlement could be found here as early as the 3rd century BC, and

Where Venice came up against its limits: Dubrovnik's cool elegance and enchanting island bays

archaeologists believe that ancient Greeks had already settled on this cove prior to that. Ancient Epidaurus disappeared amid the chaos of the Migration Period during the 7th century AD, but its inhabitants managed to flee to an island around 20 km/12.5 miles to the north that would later form the basis of the city republic of Ragusa – the later Dubrovnik. Cavtat was resettled from Ragusa during the 14th and 15th centuries, so it's no surprise that the town is reminiscent of its bigger sister.

The northern arm of Cavtat bay – the *Rat peninsula* – is shaped like a lobster claw reaching far out to sea. Its thick Mediterranean vegetation invites visitors to stroll in the shade of pines and cypresses and to bathe at one of its many enchanting coves. On the highest point of the island, the peak of *Sv. Rok,* you will find decorative gravestones from across the ages piled against each other around the distinctive *Račić Mausoleum* in the city cemetery.

Evening by the sea on Cavtat's beach which stretches along the coastline

SIGHTSEEING

OLD TOWN

Cavtat's old town extends uphill from the palm-fronted promenade of the Riva. The parish church of *Sv. Nikola* overlooks the sea, while its precious treasures are preserved in the *Pinacoteca (June–Oct Mon–Sat 10am–1pm, 4–7pm | 10 kuna)* next door. A few steps further on lies the *Rector's Palace (Knežev dvor)* with its elegant blend of Gothic and Renaissance architectural features – a miniature copy of the Dubrovnik original. In the streets behind it you will find the *Kuča Bukovac (Mon–Sat 9am–6pm, Sun 9am–2pm | 30 kuna | Bukovčeva 5 | www.kuca-bukovac. hr)*, the home of the Croatian Art Nouveau painter Vlaho Bukovac (1855–1922). The original furnishings and layout of the house (together with its ornamental garden hidden behind high walls) provide a vivid insight into bourgeois life at the time. At the end of the promenade lies the *Gospe od snijega* church and monastery. This 15th-century Renaissance complex is unfortunately closed to the public most of the time.

RAČIĆ MAUSOLEUM

The white marble mausoleum of the Račić family perched high over Cavtat is supposed to symbolise birth, life and death, and was created in 1922 by the Croatian master sculptor Ivan Meštrović for a shipping dynasty from Dubrovnik. Based on an ancient temple and watched over by caryatids, this monumental tomb dominates the city cemetery. *Mon–Sat 10am–5pm | 10 kuna*

FOOD & DRINK

ANCORA

This place is more of a bar than a restaurant, but its menu of Croatian tapas makes it a good place to go for a snack – not to mention its attractive position overlooking the harbour. *Obala Ante Starčevića 22 | no tel. | Budget*

BUGENVILA
The elegant dishes served at the Riva restaurant could be described as works of art. If you're willing to dig deep into your pocket, the degustation menu is definitely worth trying. *Obala Dr. A. Starčevića 9 | tel. 020 47 99 49 | bugenvila.eu | Expensive*

KONOBA KOLONA ◕
Anyone for swordfish carpaccio, shellfish *bužara* or aubergine tartare? Traditional Dalmatian cuisine is enriched with contemporary dishes, and everything is freshly caught by the chef himself. *Put Tihe 2 | tel. 020 47 8269 | Moderate*

SPORTS & ACTIVITIES

BEACHES
The popular beach of *Kamen mali* on the Rat peninsula (10 minutes' walk from the old town) is an idyllic rocky cove with a small, romantic bar. However, INSIDER TIP *Pasjača* beach – located 13 km/8 miles to the south-east by the village of Popovići – is still a relative secret. Set on a fine shingle cove, it nestles at the foot of a 250 m/820 ft sheer cliff.

DIVING
An absolute highlight for divers is the cargo of an ancient Greek trading ship that sank just off the coast at Cavtat. A cage has been set up to protect the amphorae on the sea floor from thieves, but the instructors at the diving centre *Epidaurum (Šetalište Žal | near the Hotel Epidaurum | tel. 020 47 13 86 | www.epidaurum.com)* have a key and allow divers to get up close to the ancient treasures.

ENTERTAINMENT

KAMEN MALI
This beach bar is the place to be for drinks and sushi on the Riva, and plays music until the early hours. *Daily 8am–1am | Obala Dr. A. Starčevića 16*

WHERE TO STAY

CAVTAT
This mid-range hotel on Tiha bay features modern furnishings, a private beach and a chic infinity pool. *92 rooms | Tiha 8 | tel. 020 20 20 00 | www.hotel-cavtat.hr | Moderate*

SUPETAR
This charming hotel located on the Riva in the old town is a good spot for travel-

MARCO POLO HIGHLIGHTS

★ Fortifications
Walk around the enormous walls surrounding Dubrovnik's old town for a unique perspective on the city → p. 80

★ Sponza Palace
This splendid city palace in Dubrovnik boasts a perfect marriage of Gothic and Renaissance elements → p. 82

★ Arboretum Trsteno
Marvel at glorious sub-tropical plants, a Renaissance villa and a jetty; enjoy the relaxing atmosphere; and take a dip in the crystal-clear sea → p. 86

★ Korčula
This picturesque town set on a peninsula boasts of being Marco Polo's birthplace → p. 90

★ Mljet
This small, romantic island is reputed to have enchanted Odysseus → p. 96

lers who want to stay close to the action. *28 rooms | Obala Dr. A. Starčevića 27 | tel. 020 47 98 33 | www.adriaticluxuryhotels. com | Moderate*

BOAT CONNECTIONS

In peak season, a boat leaves for *Dubrovnik* every hour between 10 am and 10pm, duration approx. 1 hour *(www. adriana-cavtat.hr)*.

INFORMATION

TOURIST INFO
Zidine 6 | tel. 020 479025 | www. tzcavtat-konavle.hr

WHERE TO GO

ČILIPI AND THE KONAVLE VALLEY
(143 E6) *(ω M8)*

Čilipi is the main village in the *Konavle Valley,* which stretches around 25 km/15.5 miles to the south of Cavtat, growing progressively narrower. Sheltered on its eastern flank by the Sniježnica mountain range (up to 1,234 m/4,050 ft high), the valley is richly fertile and the Konavle Valley is an important agricultural area in the otherwise sparse karst landscapes of South Dalmatia – which is why the occupation of the valley by Serbian and Montenegrin troops in 1991/1992 during the Yugoslav War had such dramatic consequences. The area was devastated, and the majority of its 10,000 inhabitants fled to Dubrovnik. Today, however, the region has recovered, as can be seen from the many newly built detached homes.
Čilipi has two main attractions. Every Sunday from Easter until October at around 11:15am, at the end of the weekly church service, the local folklore society *Linđo* performs traditional songs and dances from the Konavle region in front of the church *(45 kuna including admission to the museum)*. There is also a small market selling handicrafts, including attractive embroidery. Just these embroideries adorning traditional dress, household goods and bags are a topic of the interesting exhibition at the INSIDER TIP *ethnographic museum (Zavičajni muzej Konavla | Tue–Sat 9am–4pm, Sun 9am–1pm | 25 kuna | Beroje 49)*. We suggest that you round off your trip into the rural hinterland with a hearty meal at the restaurant *Vinica (Pridvorje | tel. 099 215 24 59 | www.konobavinica.com | Budget)*. You will need to book in advance to enjoy the peka-cooked lamb, but the other grilled meat and fish dishes on offer are also superb.
Around 17 km/10.5 miles southeast of Čilipi towers the impressive 14th century fortress of ☀ INSIDER TIP *Sokol grad (falcon town) (Dunave | April/May 10am–5pm, May–Oct 10am–7pm, Nov 10am–4pm | 40 kuna)*. The castle appears to literally grow out of the rock. Built on the remains of Illyrian and Roman sites, it was the largest fort at the time of the Dubrovnik Republic and of strategic importance because of its position on the mountain pass. From up here, the whole of Konavle stretches out beneath you. Recently re-opened after restoration, the fort is not yet overcrowded with tourists. Be particularly careful on the steep steps!

DUBROVNIK

MAP INSIDE THE BACK COVER
(143 D5) *(ω L7)* **Visitors first have to make their way past crooked city gates and massive bastions before they can fall under the spell of this bright and elegantly beautiful city (pop. 42,000).** Nonetheless, this fully preserved city wall forms a large part of Dubrovnik's

WHERE TO START?

From **Pile Gate** in the west of the old town, where the tourist info is located, you have direct access to the historic centre and the tour along the city walls. Parking is possible in **Iza Grada** along the northern city walls or at the Gradac Park west of the old town. There are buses to Pile Gate from the bus station on Gruž harbour *(Obala Ivana Pavla II)*.

charm, and visitors feel themselves transported back through the centuries to a time when Ragusa defied both the city republic of Venice and the Ottoman Empire, and was conquered by neither. Or perhaps it's more accurate to say that it played its opponents off against each other. Ragusa's strength was its tightly interlinked and far-reaching network of diplomatic and trade relations, and its military endeavours were restricted to an attempt to make the city unconquerable. Even Napoleon, who plundered Ragusa's treasures in 1806, was unable to breach the city's fortifications; the city gates were opened to him instead. Today, Dubrovnik is entirely devoted to tourism which brings both pros and cons. On the one hand, the majority of locals make their livelihood from tourists yet on the other, the quality of life in the old town suffers from the mass influx of visitors during the summer months. And it goes further: To retain its status as a World Heritage Site, Unesco has appealed to the city to cull the number of tourists. The "Pearl of the Adriatic" is becoming harder and ever more expensive to admire. The best time to visit is in the off-peak season.

SIGHTSEEING

DOMINICAN MONASTERY (DOMINIKANSKI SAMOSTAN)

This monastery situated on the approach to the Ploče Gate was founded in 1225, and in the 16th century an enchanting ● cloister was added to it. Palms and or-

The route around the city walls starts at the Pile Gate

ange trees grow in the courtyard, which is a peaceful and idyllic place. The monastery's *Gallery* is also worth a look – in particular its triptych painted by Nikola Božidarević in the early 16th century, showing St Blaise holding a model of Ragusa in his hands. *May–Oct daily 9am–6pm, winter 9am–5pm | 30 kuna | Svetog Dominika 4*

FORTIFICATIONS (GRADSKE ZIDINE) ★

The 1,940 m/6,365 ft-long *City Wall* was expanded enormously by the city fathers during the 15th/16th centuries. The best architects of the age – Juraj Dalmatinac from Zadar, Michelozzo Michelozzi from Florence and the Ragusan Paskoje Miličević – reinforced the monumental structure with five forts, 16 towers, 120 cannons and two main gates: the *Pile Gate* in the west and the *Ploče Gate* in the east. The two-hour walk around the tops of the walls forcefully conveys just how impregnable the defences were, and offers new perspectives (and photo opportunities) over the old town. The main entrance can be found next to the Pile Gate, two other access points are by *Sv. Luka* church and *Sv. Ivan Fortress*. The route runs anti-clockwise only.

● *Sv. Ivan Fortress* was built in the 14th/15th centuries to protect Ragusa's port, now known as the "Old Harbour". Here you can inspect the fortifications from the inside, as the basement contains an attractive *Aquarium (daily May–Oct 9am–7pm, July/Aug until 9pm, Nov–April Mon–Sat 9am–1pm | 60 kuna)*, displaying Mediterranean flora and fauna in 20 tanks. The rooms above contain a *Maritime Museum (Tue–Sun, Nov–March 9am–4pm, April–Oct 9am–6pm | 40 kuna)* explaining Ragusa's naval history. The bulky Renaissance *Fort Lovrijenac* stands on a 37 m/121 ft spur of rock in front of the western wall. Does it look familiar? In the fantasy TV show "Game of Thrones" it doubles as King's Landing, the capital of the Seven Kingdoms. *April/May and Aug/Sept daily 8am–6:30pm, June/July 8am–7:30pm, Oct 8am–5:30pm, Nov–March 9am–3pm | joint ticket fortifications, Sv. Ivan Fortress and Fort Lovrijenac 150 kuna, museums cost extra, joint ticket 120 kuna*

FRANCISCAN PRIORY (FRANJEVAČKI SAMOSTAN)

The monastery by the Pile Gate was founded in the 14th century, and left

GREETINGS TO THE PRINCE

Everyone is entitled to get their anger off their chest. But when this rage is directed at your boss who just happens to be a prince and you were around several hundreds of years ago, a cheeky misplaced comment could cost you your head. This did not stop the Dubrovnik Baroque poet, Junije Palmotić (1607–1657), from unleashing his unbridled hatred against a local prince in a poetic manner: in his vulgar 105-(!) verse poem entitled "Gomnaida". This tirade of insults was only published later so the prince in question probably never saw the final piece which saved the poet his life. Palmotić will however go down in Croatian literary history as the only ever poet to use at least twice as many expletives as verses in the poem.

The Great Onofrio Fountain was part of the city's water-supply system in the 15th century

in ruins by the devastating earthquake of 1667; however its fantastic cloister escaped damage almost completely, meaning that visitors can still marvel at the grotesque figures and mythical creatures that adorn its column capitals. The monks here operated a pharmacy from 1317 onwards, making it one of the oldest in Europe. It is still preserved inside the monastery in the form it took at the beginning of the 20th century. *Summer daily 9am–6pm, Nov–March 9am–5pm | 30 kuna | Placa 2 | www.godubrovnik.guide/ dubrovnikthingstodo/franciscan-church-and-monastery*

GREAT ONOFRIO FOUNTAIN (VELIKA ONOFRIJEVA FONTANA)

This polygonal fountain built by the Pile Gate in 1438 has sustained a great deal of damage over the years, and aside from its 16 cisterns (or *maškeron*) is almost devoid of ornament. It formed the end point of an eleven kilometre-long water pipe leading from a karst spring into the city – a technological masterpiece created by the architect Onofrio della Cava. Another smaller fountain also used to supply the Luža market square.

GUNDULIĆEVA POLJANA

One of the liveliest and most attractive squares in the old town; a market is held here every morning next to the cathedral and at the foot of the monument to the Ragusan poet Ivan Gundulić (1589–1638). Farmers from Konavle sell fruit, vegetables, honey and Dubrovnik's speciality: INSIDER TIP candied bitter orange peels *(arancini)*.

MUSEUM OF CONTEMPORARY ART (UMJETNIČKA GALERIJA DUBROVNIK)

Housed in the former residence of a rich ship-building family, this gallery is located just a few minutes away from the old town and showcases over 300 works of contemporary art including some of Dalmatian Art Nouveau painter Vlaho Bukovac. Splendid views of the old town

Shopping and sightseeing in one at Stradun

can be enjoyed from the sculpture terrace. *Daily 9am–8pm | joint ticket 120 kuna, valid 7 days for 8 other museums as well | Frana Supila 23 | ugdubrovnik.hr*

PLACA (STRADUN)

This 300 m/984 ft-long street – known to residents as *Placa* – runs from the Pile Gate to the former market square Luža. Its path follows that of the channel that used to separate the originally Slavic settlement of Dubrovnik on the mainland from the Romanic island of Ragusa, before being filled in during the 11th century. A devastating earthquake destroyed the city in 1667, and the reconstruction gave the Placa its uniform look, as the City Council imposed strict rules governing the floor height and appearance of the new buildings. Nowadays the marble-paved street is lined with cafés and boutiques, and in the evenings people come here to promenade along the lively *korzo*.

RECTOR'S PALACE (KNEŽEV DVOR)

Although the city governor's palace harks back to the 15th century with its typically Ragusan blend of Gothic and Renaissance styles, its current form actually dates from the 17th/18th centuries. The ground floor contains guardrooms and a dungeon, while the Rector's apartments can be seen upstairs. Each Rector was only elected for a one-month term, and during that period was not permitted to leave his quarters in order to prevent anybody from influencing his judgment. *April–Oct daily 9am–6pm, Nov–March 9am–4pm | 80 kuna | Pred dvorom 1*

RUPE ETHNOGRAPHIC MUSEUM (ETNOGRAFSKI MUZEJ RUPE)

The museum's collection of clothing and tools from Dubrovnik and the neighbouring Konavle valley is just as interesting as the building in which it is housed: an enormous 15th-century granary built directly onto the city wall, in which Ragusa used to store its supplies. *April–Oct daily 9am–6pm, winter Mon–Sat 9am–2pm | 35 kuna | Od Rupa 3*

SPONZA PALACE (PALAČA SPONZA) ★

The Placa was originally lined with buildings in the same style as this palazzo,

with Venetian Gothic ground-floor arcades and first-floor windows topped by Renaissance elements on the upper floors. Decorative, elegant, and simply perfect. The 1667 earthquake damaged the Sponza Palace, which was used as a customs house at the time; however the damage was repaired, allowing this wonderful example of Ragusan architecture to survive to the present day. Nowadays it contains the city archive, as well as a memorial to the victims of the Siege of Dubrovnik by Yugoslavian troops in 1991/1992. Nowadays it contains the city archive, as well as a memorial to the victims of the Siege of Dubrovnik by Yugoslavian troops in 1991/ 92. 114 civilian victims died during this nine-month siege. A large part of the historic buildings was destroyed and had to be re-constructed – the new bright-red roof slates symbolize this effort. Just a few streets further is the *War Photo Limited Gallery (daily 10am– 10pm | 50 kuna | Antuninska 6)* which exhibits moving war photos. Opposite the Sponza Palace stands the *Orlando Column,* erected in 1418; the statue's forearm was used to set the standard length

of the Ragusan cubit (51.2 cm/20.16 in). At the western end of the Palace is the 31 m/102 ft *Clock Tower* (1444), whose two bronze figures strike the bell every hour. The original figures are on display in the Rector's Palace.

SYNAGOGUE
Dubrovnik's Jewish community lived in the ghetto around *Žudioska ulica* ("Jewry Street") from the 15th century onwards. This simple synagogue is the only building of the old ghetto to be preserved today. Historical documents and photographs serve as a reminder of the Jewish community, the majority of whom were deported from Dubrovnik during the fascist occupation in the Second World War. Today the Jewish community counts just under 30 members. *May–Oct daily 10am–8pm, winter Mon–Fri 10am–3pm | 40 kuna | Žudioska ulica 5*

LOW BUDGET

Dubrovnik is packed with museums and monasteries to visit. The *Dubrovnik Card* offers you free or reduced-price admission, as well as free public transport.*(190 kuna/ day | www.dubrovnikcard.com)*.

Looking for good-value food in Dubrovnik? Unfortunately there aren't a lot of options, but the *Buffet Škola (Antuninska 1)* offers tasty sandwiches to suit any budget.

Seafood and fish at affordable prices? At *Barba (Boškovićeva 5 | tel. 091 2 05 34 88)* in Dubrovnik you can get them to take away – e.g. in an octopus burger *(around 40 kuna)*.

FOOD & DRINK

DUBRAVKA 1836 ⚴

High-quality Dalmatian cuisine with no surprises; what makes this place really special is its fantastic view of the city walls. *Brsalje 1 | tel. 020 42 63 19 | www.nautikarestaurants.com/dubravka-restaurant-cafe | Expensive*

KAMENICE

A Dubrovnik classic: visit during the morning to feast on oysters and champagne (the main reason to come here) while enjoying a view over the lively market. *Gundulićeva poljana 8 | tel. 020 32 36 82 | Moderate*

INSIDER TIP ▶ KOPUN

On the square in front of the Jesuit church, this place serves excellent food – including specialities from other regions such as the capon from which it takes its name. A special tip for fans: the Game of Thrones set menu. *Poljana R. Boškovića 7 | tel. 020 32 39 69 | www.restaurantkopun.com | Expensive*

NISHTA ⚫

High-quality vegan food is almost impossible to find along the coast which makes the creative dishes at this restaurant all the more special. Just a few minutes away from Stradun, this place will convince ardent carnivores. The brownies come highly recommended. *Prijeko | tel. 020 32 20 88 | www.nishtarestaurant.com | Moderate*

INSIDER TIP ▶ STARA LOŽA

The restaurant of the hotel *Prijeko Palace* attracts its guest with fine Mediterranean dining on the top floor of a Renaissance palace. You can also find a unique tapas bar here. *Prijeko 22 | tel. 020 32 11 45 | Expensive*

WANDA ⚫

A pleasant restaurant on the hyper-commercial Prijeko street where the Italian-influenced food is fresh and lavishly prepared. *Prijeko 8 | tel. 098 9 44 93 17 | www.wandarestaurant.com | Moderate*

SHOPPING

The main shopping streets are the *Placa* and the *Pred Dvorom* that branches off to the south; here you can find plenty of souvenir and fashion shops.

DEŠA

Embroidery, marmalade and honey produced by women from Konavle who were driven out and traumatised by the war. *Frana Supila 8 | in the Lazareti | desa-dubrovnik.hr*

DUBROVAČKA KUĆA

High-quality souvenirs such as excellent oil, Croatian wines and wonderful handicrafts. *Od sv. Dominika*

KOKULA

Attractive handicrafts from the region, many of which are made in-house by this family company. *Đorđićeva 6*

SPORTS & LEISURE

KAYAKING

Paddling around the old town in a kayak makes for a wonderfully peaceful way to enjoy the views. Tours start from the cove beneath *Fort Lovrijenac*. *Adventure Dubrovnik (duration approx. 3 hours | 250 kuna | Sv. Križa 3 | tel. 098 53 15 16 | www.adventuredubrovnik.com)*

BEACHES

Close to the old town lie the coves of the island *Lokrum* (shingle and rock), as well as the sand/shingle beach *Ban-*

je near the Lazareti (Ploče Gate). Here you can also find the *East-West-Beach-club (ew-dubrovnik.com)* with its luxurious loungers (approx. 100 kuna per lounger) and DJ sets. Other beaches are available in the hotel quarters in *Lapad* and *Babin Kuk,* they may be subject to an admission fee.

ENTERTAINMENT

BUŽA I AND BUŽA II
These two bars on the rocks in front of the southern city wall are the places to go in Dubrovnik. You won't find a more relaxed place to enjoy a drink with a view of the sea. To get here, just follow the "cold drinks" signs. *Daily 8am–2am*

CULTURE CLUB REVELIN
Enjoy live gigs by Croatian pop stars and DJ parties over two floors in this historic fortress. *Daily 11pm–6am | Sv. Dominika | at the Ploče Gate | www.clubrevelin.com*

LAZARETI
This former quarantine for Plague victims has been transformed into a cultural centre containing art galleries and a nightclub. Parties and live concerts are organised to suit every music taste in this historic setting. *Frana Supila 8 | www.lazareti.com*

TROUBADOUR HARD JAZZ CAFÉ
The classic among the many café-bars on this square in the old town. Formerly devoted to jazz fans, nowadays it has opened itself up to a broader set of musical tastes. *Daily 10am–2am | Bunićeva poljana 2*

WHERE TO STAY

BELLEVUE ☆
Each and every room offers a fantastic panorama over the open sea, while the restaurant and service are perfect. Guests can also relax in the small spa with pool and shingle beach. *91 rooms |*

The Troubadour Café is popular among fans of jazz and live music

Pera Čingrije 7 | tel. 020 43 08 30 | www. adriaticluxuryhotels.com | Expensive

BERKELEY HOTEL

This friendly mid-range hotel is located in Gruž, close to the harbour and the bus station. *24 rooms | Andrije Hebranga 116A | tel. 020 49 41 60 | www.berkeleyhotel.hr | Moderate*

FRESH SHEETS

A cheerful and colourful hostel in the old town, offering one double room and several dorms. *16 beds | Ulica Svetog Šimuna 15 | tel. 091 799 20 86 | www.freshsheetshostel.com | Budget*

PRIJEKO PALACE

Admittedly, this place is only for travellers with a generous budget: in this Renaissance palace in the old town the interior of each room was designed by a different artist. Even if you don't want to stay here then you should at least admire the exterior of the building! *9 rooms, 5 apts. | Prijeko 22 | tel. 020 32 11 45 | www. prijekopalace.com | Expensive*

ST. JOSEPH´S

The charming and tastefully decorated suites are the perfect haven to escape the hustle and bustle in the old town. *6 rooms | Sv. Josipa 3 | tel. 020 43 20 89 | www.stjosephs.hr | Expensive*

TRANSPORT LINKS

Several bus routes run back and forth between the hotel districts of *Lapad* and *Babin Kuk,* as well as from the *Gruž* harbour to the *old town* (mostly arriving at the *Pile Gate*). Ferries to *Lokrum* leave once per hour from the *Old Harbour,* while boats to the *Elaphiti Islands* depart from *Gruž* three times a day *(www. jadrolinija.hr)*.

INFORMATION

TOURIST INFO

Pile | Brsalje 5 | tel. 020 32 38 87 | experience.dubrovnik.hr

WHERE TO GO

ARBORETUM TRSTENO ★

(143 D5) *(ᗰ L7)*

A magical park created in the 15th century at the behest of a Ragusan noble family at their similarly well-preserved *Summer Palace* around 18 km/11 miles to the north. Palm, eucalyptus, laurel, bougainvillea, oak and Aleppo pine surround statues, fountains and a villa. Its port used to be a docking point for ships from Ragusa and other cities. Today, it's pleasure boats. If you brought your bathing costume then take a INSIDER TIP dip in front of this opulent backdrop! A number of scenes for "Game of Thrones" were filmed on this location, which served as the palace garden of House Baratheon. *May–Oct daily 7am–7pm, Nov–April 8am–4pm | 50 kuna | Potok 20 | www.tzdubrovnik.hr/lang/en/get/prirodne_znamenitosti/53065/arboretum_trsteno.html*

LOKRUM (143 D5) *(ᗰ L8)*

This tiny island lies in front of the Old Harbour. Its green vegetation is due to the Habsburg Archduke Maximilian, who had the island planted with exotic trees and shrubs in the middle of the 19th century, and also introduced peacocks. Today, the island is an area of natural protection, and is a popular bathing spot among Dubrovnik's residents – its shady coves quickly fill up on summer weekends. Series fans are drawn by the small *Game of Thrones Museum (daily 11am–7pm | admission free)* inside the Benedictine abbey. A ferry service operates every 30 to 60 minutes from the Old Harbour.

Three minutes by cable car or 1.5 hours on foot: many paths lead up to the summit of Srd

NERETVA DELTA (142 C3–4) *(🕮 K6)*

The coastal mountain range opens up between *Neum* and *Ploče* to make room for the 280 km/174 mile long Neretva River. At the mouth to the Adriatic Sea, this river flows into another delta, known as the Neretva Delta. In "California in Croatia" mandarins grow on trees like in the Garden of Eden. You can even roll up your sleeves and join in the INSIDER TIP *mandarin harvest.* Day pickers come from Dubrovnik and Makarska to lend a hand with the picking. The frogs and eels from this former swamp region were once seen as poor-man's food and are today sold as a delicacy. Try a Neretva stew *(brudet)* in the restaurant *Đuda i Mate (Vid | tel. 020 68 75 00 | djudjaimate.hr | Moderate)*.

SRĐ 🌿 (143 D5) *(🕮 L7)*

This 412 m/1,352 ft hill is both Dubrovnik's most beautiful viewpoint and a memorial to the Yugoslavian War in 1991/1992. The 60-man unit stationed in *Fort Imperial* on its summit put up a spirited resistance to the much larger attacking forces during the Siege of Dubrovnik, and a museum *(winter daily 8am–4pm, summer 8am–6pm | 30 kuna)* inside the fort tells the story. Both the summit and the museum can be reached by car, on foot, or by means of a modern cable car *(Nov–March daily 9am–4pm, April/May/Oct 9am–8pm, Sept 9am–10pm, June–Aug 9am–midnight | return trip 140 kuna | Petra Krešimira 4 | www.dubrovnikcablecar. com)*. The city administration has given their approval for the development of hotels, villas and a golf course on the top of the hill, despite bitter resistance from environmental campaigners.

ELAPHITI ISLANDS

(143 D5) *(🕮 L7)* **A string of 13 islands – three of which are inhabited – lie one after another along the coast of**

South Dalmatia. The Greek sailors who traded along the coast called them the Deer Islands *(elaphos* meaning "deer"). *Koločep, Lopud* and *Šipan* are particularly attractive to individualist visitors thanks to their rich vegetation, tiny island villages and secluded coves.

Wealthy ship owners and nobles from Ragusa erected palaces and fortresses on the islands during the city state's golden age. Most of these have now fallen into disrepair, but the examples that have been preserved are hugely impressive. The Elaphiti Islands are largely car-free, making them the perfect destination for visitors who want to get away from it all and explore isolated routes and trails.

KOLOČEP (143 D5) (*ⓘ L7*)

The island of Koločep (pop. 165) measures 2.4 km², and of the three inhabited Elaphiti Islands it is the one most oriented towards tourism. Nonetheless, the largely English holidaymakers that come here mainly find accommodation in privately rented apartments. An attractive 3-km/1.9 mile walking trail runs through olive groves and pine forests between the villages of Gornje Čelo and Donje Čelo. The vegetation here proliferates largely unchecked, although traces of former Ragusan gardens and ruined villas can still be found in many places. The path along the ↘↙ rugged north-west coast is also wonderful, and offers enthralling and constantly changing views. Guests on the terrace of the enchanting restaurant*Villa Ruža (May–Sept only | Donje Čelo | tel. 020 75 70 30 | www.villa-ruza.com | Moderate)* will experience a wonderful atmosphere around sunset. The *Kalamota Island Resort (144 rooms | Donje Čelo | tel. 020 312150 | www.kalamotaislandresort.com | Expensive)* provides an all-inclusive offer that will particularly appeal to visitors without children.

Information: via the tourist information in Dubrovnik.

Many visitors to Dubrovnik also travel to Koločep, the smallest of the Elaphiti Islands

LOPUD ● (143 D5) (*∅ L7*)

The west-facing village of *Lopud* (pop. 400) is the arrival point for ferries, and welcomes visitors with a picturesque view of its oval harbour lined with monasteries, palaces and old captain's houses. Renovation works at the Franciscan monastery have been underway for years now, and the former *Rector's Palace* and the Palace of the Đorđić-Mayneri family with its palm garden are in a sad state of repair. A contrast is provided by the INSIDERTIP installation "Your black horizon" by the Icelandic artist Oliafur Eliasson *(mid-May–Sept daily 10am–7pm | admission free)* which stands between the ruins.

An attractive walking trail runs past the Hotel Lafodia to the *Benešin rat* cape, where a ☀ *pavillon* offers views of the neighbouring island Šipan. Lopud has a major asset in its child- and family-friendly sandy beach of *Šumj* on the northern coast. You can get to the beach in a twenty-minute walk that takes you across the island, and facilities include parasol rental and a small snack bar.

At the hotel-restaurant *Glavović (April–Oct | 12 rooms | Obala Ivana Kuljevana | tel. 020 75 93 59 | www.hotel-glavovic.hr | Moderate)* you can dine on a cool terrace overlooking the sea. The enchanting *La Villa (6 rooms | Obala Ivana Kuljevana 33 | tel. 091 3 22 01 26 | www.lavilla.com.hr | Expensive)* is also recommended.

Information: *Tourist Info (May–Oct Sat–Thu 8am–1pm, 5–7pm | Obala Ivana Kuljevana 12 | Lopud | tel. 020 75 90 86)*

ŠIPAN (143 D5) (*∅ L7*)

Measuring 14.5 km² and with 500 inhabitants, Šipan is the largest and most populous of the Elaphiti Islands. The island used to be a base for Ragusan nobles and wealthy ship owners, but almost all of its 60 villas and palaces have fallen into disrepair, as have the many old Croatian chapels that testify to an early Slavic settlement. Their ruins are scarcely visible under the rampant vegetation. The two villages of *Šipanska Luka* in the east and *Suđurađ* in the west are linked by a fertile and intensively farmed karst valley, along which the island's bus service runs in coordination with the ferry arrival times. Unlike Lopud, Šipan lacks any wide beachy coves – visitors will instead need to wander along the coast to one of the small rocky coves, or simply jump off the rocks into the sea.

In *Suđurađ* you can gain a sense of the former glory of this island when you look at the restored 16th-century *Country Residence* of the Stjepović-Skočibuha family. Unfortunately, the villa can only be visited as part of an organised excursion from Dubrovnik. If you miss out then you can console yourself with freshly caught fish specialities and charming service at the ☀ restaurant *Tri Sestre (May–Sept | Suđurađ 1C | tel. 020 75 80 87 | Expensive)*. A trip on the island bus service or a one-hour walk will take you to *Šipanska Luka*, which lies in a deep cove and is centred on an attractive park surrounded by cafés. Here, the restaurant *Kod Marka (May–Sept | tel. 020 75 80 07 | Expensive)* comes particularly recommended. The chef won't tell you what exactly is on the menu, but you can guarantee it will be fresh and delicious. The Hotel Šipan *(75 rooms | tel. 020 36 19 01 | www.hotel-sipan.com | Moderate)* offers stylishly designed rooms, and you can also rent out kayaks and mountain bikes.

BOAT CONNECTIONS

Passenger ferries to *Lopud* and *Suđurađ* leave from *Gruž/Dubrovnik* harbour four times a day during the week and twice

...ay on Sundays (four times a day ...ng July/August). Car ferries sail twice ...day (see *www.jadrolinija.hr* for both). Numerous travel agencies offer day-trips taking in all three islands, leaving from Dubrovnik.

KORČULA

(141 D–E 5–6) *(Ⓜ H–J7)* **The island of Korčula (176 km², pop. 17,000) is just under 50 km/31 miles long, and as one of Dalmatia's most important regions for olive oil and wine production it has a strong emphasis on agriculture – particularly in its eastern half. The west features plenty of narrow coves, surrounded by pine and holm oaks. The island's capital, also called Korčula, is a charming miniature version of Dubrovnik.**

The lengthy periods of foreign domination that punctuate the history of Dalmatia are plain to see in the towns on the island – especially Korčula. The island was governed by Venice from 1427 until it was conquered by Napoleon in 1797. This led to a certain degree of tension, however, as the neighbouring peninsula of *Pelješac* (see p. 93) belonged to Venice's main competitor Ragusa – and the border between the two ran through the 1.3 km/0.8 mile-wide strait *Pelješki kanal* directly in front of Korčula town (and is now popular with windsurfers). The island's superb olives oils and wines – including the fruity white varieties *Pošip* and *Grk* and the fiery red *Plavac Mali* – can be sampled on Discovery Tour 4 (see p. 110).

PLACES ON KORČULA

BLATO (141 D5) *(Ⓜ H7)*
Blato (pop. 4,000) is known for its kilometre-long boulevard of lime trees. The main square features a freestanding

Loggia and a *parish church* (14th century) with a side chapel dedicated to the town's patron St Vincenca. On her saint's day on April 28th the local folklore group performs the traditional *kumpanija* sword dance in front of the church.

The delicious meals served in the cosy inner courtyard of the *Konoba Zlinje (Ulica 85 6/1 | tel. 020 85 10 50 | Budget)* are based on products from the region, and we particularly recommend the freshly caught fish.

KORČULA ★ ● (141 E5) *(Ⓜ J7)*
Viewed from the sea, Korčula looks like the foredeck of a ship protruding into the sea on its peninsula, and intersected from north to south by the main street *Korčulanskog statua.* A series of lanes branch off from it on the left and right, all leading to the sea. Fresh easterly and westerly winds blow through the town, acting like a natural air conditioning system. Although Korčula (pop. 5,600) received its forward-looking layout during the 13th century, it already had a long and turbulent history behind it involving previous Greek, Roman and Slavic settlements. The late Medieval and Renaissance buildings of the town are remarkably well preserved.

The main street leads gently uphill past the *Town Hall* and the *Sv. Mihovil chapel* (both dating from 1525) to its highest point, the *Trg. Sv. Marko* (St Mark's Square). This square is dominated by the 15th-century *Katedrala Sv. Marka,* whose portal features two Gothic lions. Inside the church, an early Tintoretto painting, late-Gothic masonry and a modern bronze of *Sv. Vlaho* by Ivan Meštrović contribute to a harmonic overall effect. Next to the cathedral, the 19th-century *Bishop's Palace (May–Sept Mon–Sat 9am–7pm, Oct 9am–2pm | 25 kuna)*

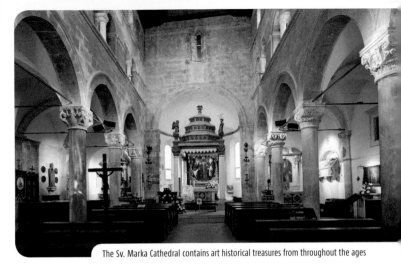

The Sv. Marka Cathedral contains art historical treasures from throughout the ages

contains a rich selection of ecclesiastical treasures and paintings. The *Renaissance Palace Gabrieli* diagonally opposite is home to the *City Museum (Oct–March daily 10am–2pm, April–June daily 10am–1pm, July-Sept daily 9am–9pm | 20 kuna)* which displays archaeological artefacts, naval instruments, the household of a Renaissance family and much more besides.

There are plenty of other noble palaces to be seen as you stroll through the streets of the town, and inevitably you will also come across a late-Gothic ruin: the *Marco Polo House (Kuća Marka Pola).* The famous explorer of China is said to have been born here in 1254, but there is little proof beyond the fact that "Dapolo" is a common surname on the island. The *Marko Polo muzej (daily April, May 10am–3pm, June–Sept 9am–11pm, Oct, Nov 10am–3pm | 60 kuna | Plokata 14. travnja 1921)* is much clearer, with dioramas and an accompanying audio guide explaining the different stages of Marco Polo's life.

At the *Aterina (Trg Korčulanskih klesara i kipara 1 | tel. 091 9 86 18 56 | Expensive)* the personable chef demonstrates his talent with modern interpretations of Dalmatian cuisine.

Local works of art are a special souvenir to take back home: The painter Abel Brči´exhibits the colourful side of Korčula in his *studio (daily 10am–10pm | Ulica Banicevica | abel-art.net).*

⊙ *Komparak (Plokota 19 | tel. 091 4 34 34 13)* sells genuine regional produce such as fig jam and honey and the owner is only too happy to tell you all about his bees. You can also visit the bee hives, olive groves and animals as well as taste some of the food. Guided tours are available in English. In the evenings, the perfect place to watch the sunset is the restaurant at the casual lounge bar *Maksimilijan Garden (Sveti Nikola | tel. 091 170 25 67 | Budget–Moderate).*

For a nostalgic stay in comfortable, ultra-modern surroundings, visit the *Korčula De La Ville (20 rooms | Obala Dr.*

Franje Tuđmana 5 | tel. 020 72 63 36 | www.korcula-hotels.com | *Moderate)* which was renovated in 2015. Situated at the edge of the old town, it enjoys a beautiful view of the sea.
Information: *Tourist Info (Obala Dr. Franje Tuđmana 4 | tel. 020 71 57 01 | www.visitkorcula.eu)*

Spoilt for choice in Lumbarda: sunbathing, boating or a swim to the nearby island?

🌍 *Villa Sokol (3 apts. | Lumbarda 44 | tel. 098 3441 82 | www.korcula-adventures.com | Moderate)*, whose owners take sustainability very seriously by using only recycled paper and taking part in reforestation initiatives, for example. The agrotourism company 🌍 *Agroturizam Bire (tel. 020 71 20 07 | www.bire.hr)* also practises sustainable viticulture

LUMBARDA (141 E5–6) (*ⓜ J7)*

Greek colonists from the island of *Vis* founded Lumbarda (pop. 1,200) as early as the 4th century BC. During the 14th and 15th centuries, nobles from Korčula erected country homes here, and a few of these restored Renaissance castles can still be seen among the green vineyards that produce a fine white wine called *Grk*. The small harbour and historical centre are surrounded by attractive coves where visitors can bathe – including the large, popular sandy beach in the cove of *Pržina*. Accommodation is primarily in private rooms and apartments, such as the

and follows strict ecological criteria to produce its wines (*Grk* and *Plavac Mali*). The *Konoba More (Bilin Zal | tel. 020 71 20 68 | Moderate)* serves grilled meat and fish in the romantic setting of a terrace overlooking the sea.
Take a detour to *Žrnovo* (8 km/5miles away) where you can try the regional pasta speciality *Žrnovski makaruni* – the best is the homemade variety rolled by hand in the family-owned *Konoba Belin (Žrnovo 50 | reservation recommended: tel. 091 5 03 92 58 | Moderate)*. You can also try your hand at pasta rolling in the **INSIDER TIP** cookery course held at the

Konoba (180 kuna per person including food, English is also spoken). The 400-year old recipe is celebrated every August at the Makarunada festival.

VELA LUKA (141 D5) (*ɯ H7*)

The harbour of Korčula's second largest settlement (pop. 4,500) points towards the west, opening out onto the open sea. Of the multiple shipyards formerly found here, only one managed to find an international market: the *Montmontaža Greben,* where lifeboats are built. The *Museum (summer Mon–Fri 8am–3pm, Sat 9am–1pm | 15 kuna)* documents the archaeological discoveries that were made in the nearby cave *Vela spilja (www.velaspila.hr),* with artefacts dating back to the Neolithic period over 20,000 years ago. With permission from the museum it is possible to visit the cave, located around 2 km/1.2 mile away.

The beaches close to the town are not particularly noteworthy, but a trip to the neighbouring island of INSIDER TIP *Proizd* is a must: its turquoise waters are among the most beautiful in Croatia. Get there via water taxi or by hiring a kayak or motor boat *(Vela Luka Rent | kayak 220 kuna/day, boat from 350 kuna/day | tel. 098 9 54 03 88 | velalukarent. com).* You can then round off your day by dining on fresh fish and shellfish in the *Konoba Lučica (Ulica 51 | tel. 020 8136 73 | Moderate).*

Information: *Tourist Info (Obala 3 br. 19 | tel. 020 8136 19 | www.tzvelaluka.hr)*

BOAT CONNECTIONS

From *Korčula (town)* several times daily to *Orebić* on *Pelješac (www.medplov. hr). Split–Hvar–Korčula* are connected by catamaran, *Split–Vela Luka–Lastovo* by car ferry *(all www.jadrolinija.hr).*

WHERE TO GO

LASTOVO (142 A5) (*ɯ H–J7*)

Visitors to this island to the south of Korčula will feel like they've reached the edge of the world. Attractive coves, crystal-clear water, verdant Mediterranean greenery, olive groves and three small villages with around 800 inhabitants make this a calm, relaxing place where you can get away from it all. Because it lies at the centre of a protected archipelago of 44 islands, Lastovo is the base for the *Lastovo National Park (www. pp-lastovo.hr).* This nature reserve is an undiscovered INSIDER TIP divers' paradise with its steep cliffs and diverse marine life. Trips can be organised through *Diving Center Ankora (Zaklopatica 46 | tel. 020 80 11 70 | lastovo-diving-ankora.com).* Visit the main village of *Lastovo* to see the island's typical chimneys, whose size and rich detailing testify to the former prosperity of the houses' owners. The best beach is *Skrivena luka,* the "hidden harbour" on the south coast. Accommodation is available from private landlords or in the island hotel *Solitudo (72 rooms | Pasadur | tel. 020 80 21 00 | www.hotel-solitudo.com | Moderate).*

Information: *Tourist Info (Pjevor | tel. 020 80 10 18 | www.tz-lastovo.hr)*

PELJEŠAC

(142 A–C 4–5) (*ɯ J–K 6–7*) **The peninsula of Pelješac is connected to the mainland by just a narrow isthmus. Like on the island of Korčula, which runs almost parallel to Pelješac, the farmers here primarily produce wine and olives.** The acquisition of the island by Ragusa in 1333 was something of a coup for the city state as it provided a base situated directly opposite Korčula, which belonged to its

rival Venice. Ragusa secured this precious territory as part of the mainland with a seven-kilometre defensive wall equipped with three forts, 41 towers, seven bastions, four ramparts and a moat – creating Europe's largest fortification in the process. The wall closed off overland access to both the peninsula and the valuable salt works near Veliki Ston.

The 65 km/40 miles-long Pelješac (pop. 10,000) is very sparsely populated. Beaches and holiday resorts can mainly be found along the flat northern coast, whereas the south coast features rugged cliffs that drop into the sea. A number of small roads carved boldly into the rock face or running through tunnels under it lead to tiny wine-growing villages, where one of the most famous of Dalmatia's wines, *Dingač,* is produced in spite of the stony, barren soils. You can even spot jackals prowling over the vineyards in the early morning. You can meet the vintners and olive farmers on Discovery Tour 4 (see p. 110).

are great for children, especially *Trstenica* beach, while active visitors will relish the thrill of racing down the *Pelješki kanal* strait on a surfboard with the steady wind of the Maestral at their backs.

The monastery *Gospa od Anđela (in summer Mon–Sat 9am–noon, 4–7pm | 20 kuna | Celestinov put 6)* built on a hill overlooking the town during the 15th century provides a reminder of the cold war between the rival maritime powers of Venice and Ragusa. From here, Ragusan lookouts would spy on the goings-on in Venetian Korčula. An atmospheric cloister, a Renaissance relief of the Madonna and child by Nikola Firentinac, and the tranquil cemetery containing the graves of sea captains are all well worth a look.

The chef at the Restaurant *Babilon (Đivovićeva 2 | tel. 020 713352 | Moderate)* has a good understanding of classic Dalmatian cuisine. The view from the res-

PLACES ON PELJEŠAC

OREBIĆ (142 B4) *(ⓜ J7)*

This town (pop. 2,000) at the foot of the 961 m/3,153 ft mountain Sv. Ilija has a proud history as the base of a significant merchant fleet, which boasted over 60 ships during the 19th century. The captains of the ships invested their profits in prestigious villas, in whose gardens they planted exotic souvenirs from their journeys across the world. Memories of this era are preserved by the *maritime museum (Pomorski muzej | Mon–Fri 7am–8pm, Sat/Sun 6–8pm, winter Mon–Fri 7am–3pm | 15 kuna | Trg Mimbelli).* Modern Orebić is a much sleepier town, but that just adds to its charms. The attractive and shallow shingle beaches to the west and north-east of the village

taurant ✹ *Panorama (in summer only, from 5pm | Celestinov put | no tel.| Moderate)* on the road leading up the monastery is genuinely stunning. Grilled dishes make up most of the menu here.

Modern comfort and a huge programme of entertainment can be found at the all-inclusive *Aminess Grand Azur Hotel (184 rooms | Kralja Petra Krešimira IV 107 | tel. 020 79 80 00 | www.aminess.com/hr/aminess-grand-azur-hotel | Moderate)* while self-catering fans will love the beautiful *Villa Melita (12 apts. | Kneza Domagoja 47 | tel. 020 713056 | www.orebic-ferien.com | Budget)* with its verdant garden.

The neighbouring village of *Viganj* is a Mecca for wind- and kitesurfers. The water sport base INSIDER TIP ▶ *Water Donkey (tel. 091 152 0258 | www.windsurfing-kitesurfing-viganj.com)* rents out surfing equipment, as well as bikes *(100 kuna/day)* and stand-up paddleboards or kayaks *(135 kuna/day)*. After a full day of activities you can party the night away in the bar *Karmela 2*.

Information: *Tourist Info (Zrinsko Frankopanska 2 | tel. 020 713718 | www.visitorebic-croatia.hr)*

STON (142 C5) (ⓜ K7)

Ston – which consists of the two villages of *Veliki* (Greater) and *Mali* (Lesser) Ston – is where the Pelješac peninsula joins the mainland on an isthmus measuring only 1,500 m/1 mile across. Both villages are encircled by a 14th-century *defensive wall (April/May, Aug/Sept daily 8am–6:30pm, June/July 8am–7:30pm, Oct 8am–5:30pm, Nov–March 8am–3pm | 50 kuna | citywallsdubrovnik.hr/bastina/stonske-zidine)* that climbs steeply over the hills that lie between them. This monumental structure was severely damaged by an earthquake in 1996, but thanks to renovation works visitors can now walk

Everything under control: Ston's fortification walls protected the town from pilferers and salt thieves

5.5 km/3.4 miles of the walls. However, it is best to avoid doing so under the heat of the midday sun, as there is absolutely no shade to be found along the route. The *salt works (summer daily 10am–7pm, winter 7am–2pm | 15 kuna | Pelješki put 1 | www.solanaston.hr)* here still produce salt using traditional evaporation methods, while the mussels and oysters cultivated in the shallow waters before Mali Ston are served freshly prepared at *Bota Šare (Mali Ston | tel. 020 75 44 82 | www. bota-sare.hr | Expensive)*. The *campsite Prapratno (960 pitches | Prapratno | tel. 020 75 40 00 | www.duprimorje.hr | Budget)* is located 3 km/1.9 mile to the south of Veliki Ston on its very own idyllic cove, complete with a brilliant white shingle beach. Even non-campers will want to pitch a tent when they see this beautiful spot.

Information: *Tourist Info (Pelješki put | Veliki Ston | tel. 020 75 44 52 | www.ston.hr*

BOAT CONNECTIONS

Boats travel from *Orebić* to *Korčula* (town) several times a day *(www.me dplov.hr)*. Five car ferries per day leave from *Prapratno* to *Sobra* on *Mljet* during the summer *(www.jadrolinija.hr)*.

WHERE TO GO

MLJET ★ (142 B–C5) (*ш K7*)

Mljet's history starts with Odysseus, who was allegedly detained here by Calypso. There followed successive waves of Romans and Illyrians, and although the island lies a long way from the coast, it was settled in the 12th century by Benedictine monks from Puglia. The western half of the island (pop. 1,100) is a *National Park (admission 70 kuna, in peak season 125 kuna | Pristanište 2 | Goveđari-Mljet | tel. 020 74 40 41 | www.np-mljet. hr)* and subject to environmental protec-

FOR BOOKWORMS & FILM BUFFS

Croatia: A Nation Forged in War – President Franjo Tudjman spoke of the Croats' "thousand-year-old dream of independence". Marcus Tanner, former Balkan correspondent of The Independent, looks at the story of the Croats from the early Middle Ages and describes how this dream finally came true in the 1990s.

Black Lamb and Grey Falcon – Rebecca West, a redoubtable Englishwoman, and her banker husband travelled round Yugoslavia in the 1930s. She recorded her impressions in a fascinating account, which includes some enchanting passages on, for example, Diocletian's palace in Split.

Winnetou 1–3 – Lex Barker as Old Shatterhand with French actor Pierre Brice as his helper, an Apache chief, in classic precursors to the spaghetti western genre that were filmed on this coast, for example in Paklenica Gorge, at the Krka cascades near Skradin and in Dubrovnik's hinterland.

Svecenikova djeca (The Priest's Children) – Very amusing feature film by the Croatian director Vinko Brešan (2014): a comedy about the church, morals, everyday life on an island and... condoms, set on an unnamed island in the Adriatic.

Pure nature: canoeists paddle across the Malo lake on the hilly island of Mljet

tion. Mljet has a varied landscape, with its rugged south coast contrasting with the many coves dotted along the north coast. There is a lot to see underwater as well – in 2017, amphorae dating back to the 1st century were discovered. Divers are invited to dive under the netting (in place to protect the treasures from being stolen) to admire the findings. The ports of *Sobra*, *Polače* and *Pomena* and the other villages on the island give the impression that time has stood still here. Mljet is still a destination for individualists, and accommodation is found primarily in private rooms.

The main attraction of the National Parks in the thickly forested west are the salt lakes *Veliko* and *Malo jezero,* the latter with the Benedictine monastery of *Sv. Marija* on an island accessible by ferry: boats leave from *Pristanište* or from the *Mali most* bridge every hour from 9am until 7pm during the summer. The small complex was built in the 12th century but now has a Renaissance style, and

the restaurant *Melita (Otok sv. Marije | Veliko jezero | tel. 020 74 41 45 | Moderate)* lies romantically within its walls. A short walk will take you past the picturesque cemetery.

Bikes and boats for a tour around or on the lakes can be rented from *Radulj Tours (tel. 098 42 80 74)* by the *Mali most* bridge, and scooters are available for 250 kuna/day at *Mini Brun (Sobra 33 | tel. 020 74 50 84 | www.rent-a-car-scooter-mljet.hr)* in *Sobra*. From *Polače,* you can hike up the highest hill on the island, ⚡ *Montokuc* (253 m/830 ft). Here you can enjoy stunning views over Korčula, Lastovo and Pelješac before returning to Polače past Veliko jezero and Pristanište (around 3 hours, clearly signposted).Mljet's ⊘ eco hotel *Soline 6 (4 studios | tel. 020 74 40 24 | www.soline6.com | Moderate)* can be found on the eastern end of Veliko jezero. Its solar-powered heating, bio-composting plant, passive cooling system and waste reprocessing facility ensure that its impact on nature is kept to a minimum.

DISCOVERY TOURS

① DALMATIA AT A GLANCE

START: ① Zadar **END:** ㉗ Split Distance: ➡ 1,170 km/727 miles	**11 days** Driving time (without stops) 26–36 hrs depending on ferries

COSTS: approx. 9,600 kuna (petrol, ferries, fees, room & board)
WHAT TO PACK: swim gear and water shoes, sun protection

IMPORTANT TIPS: during the peak season, expect long waits for the car ferries! Don't forget your car registration because you will need it to cross the border near Neum (Bosnia and Herzegovina)! Dubrovnik–Lokrum ferries depart daily from April–Nov every half hour from 9am to 6pm, the trip takes approx. 10 min.; book your rafting tour in ⑩ **Cetina Gorge** 1 to 5 days in advance *(www.rafting-cetina.com)*

Would you like to explore the places that are unique to this region? Then the Discovery Tours are just the thing for you – they include terrific tips for stops worth making, breathtaking places to visit, selected restaurants and fun activities. It's even easier with the Touring App: download the tour with map and route to your smartphone using the QR Code on pages 2/3 or from the website address in the footer below – and you'll never get lost again even when you're offline.

TOURING APP

→ p. 2/3

Follow this tour south along the Dalmatian coast to some of the most attractive harbour towns and national parks. You'll visit world-famous cultural landmarks and pretty bays with beaches where you can take a refreshing swim. On the way back north from Dubrovnik, hop from one island to the next on the ferries and experience the magic of this stretch of coastline.

After breakfast, leave the lively town of ❶ **Zadar** → p. 44 behind and **follow the Adria Magistrale E65 to the southeast**. After 30 km (18.6 miles), stop in **Biograd na Moru** → p. 32 and plan your first bathing stops here. Enjoy the

DAY 1
❶ Zadar
30 km/18.5 mi

2 Dražica

4 km/2.5 mi

3 Resort

5 km

4 Konoba Pakoštanac

DAY 2

50 km/31 mi

5 Šibenik

30 km/18.5 mi

sea on the popular beach of **2 Dražica** on the Biograd Riviera or directly on **Crvena Luka** bay – with a sandy stretch. Check into the **3 Resort** → p. 34 of the same name. In the afternoon, you'll have time for a **trip to Pakoštane a few kilometres to the south** to try the excellent local Babić red wine at **4 Konoba Pakoštanac** → p. 36.

Get an early start the next day around 9am, if possible. **Drive 50 km (31 miles) along the Adria Magistrale to 5 Šibenik** → p. 39 with its fascinating Renaissance-style architecture. Enjoy a tasty lunch and the view of the cathedral at the restaurant **Gradska Vijećnica**. The D56 will **lead you 30 km (18.6 miles) further away from the coast**

DISCOVERY TOURS

to Skradin and ⑥ **Krka National Park** → p. 109, which is a paradise for hikers thanks to the river of the same name that flows through the gorges and over the cascades. **After returning to Šibenik, take the E65 50 km (31 miles) to the south to** ⑦ **Trogir** → p. 70 whose **Sv. Lovro Cathedral** is graced with a Romanesque portal. The best place to spend the night is the hotel **Pašike** in the old town and dine in the restaurant **Alka** in the evening.

The E65 runs from Trogir along the route of the castles → p. 69, which earned its name thanks to the fortress-like constructions from the 15th and 16th century that can be seen off in the distance. **After 30 km (18.5 miles), you will reach** ⑧ **Split** → p. 65 with its museums, shops, cafés and **Diocletian's palace**, which you simply must see. Settle in for the night **29 km (18 miles) to the south on the E65 in** ⑨ **Omiš** → p. 64. The next morning, it is time for a little outdoor adventure: the agency Kentona → p. 65 organizes rafting tours down the ⑩ **Cetina Gorge** → p. 65. After this wet and wild trip, treat yourself to a hearty meal at the water mill ⑪ **Radmanove mlinice** → p. 65, a popular destination in the Mosor Mountains.

After spending another night in Omiš, head out the next day **along the coast via the Adria Magistrale to the south until you come to the Makarska Riviera** with its enchanting ⑫ **Dugi rat beach** → p. 63. Before you embark on the next (longer) stretch of the tour, bury your feet in the sand for a bit. **After about 90 km (56 miles) on the coastal road, you will have to pass through the Neum Corridor**, a 5-km stretch of the road (3 miles) through Bosnian territory (passport and customs checks!). Once you have arrived in ⑬ **Dubrovnik** → p. 78, where you will stay for two nights, take a leisurely evening stroll, a *korzo*, through the wonderfully-preserved **old town** and splurge on dinner at **Stara Loža**. Later on, enjoy drinks at the **Buža Bars**. On day 2 in Dubrovnik, walk along the high city walls around the **old town** and stop at the most important sights such as the **Rector's palace**. In the afternoon, **take a boat to the island of** ⑭ **Lokrum** → p. 86 and find yourself a pretty bay for a swim. **Return to town** for dinner and take your pick among the restaurants – how about cosy ⑮ **Wanda**?

After breakfast, it's time to leave Dubrovnik behind. **Follow the E65 northwards for 21 km (13 miles) to the** ⑯ **Arboretum** → p. 86 in Trsteno, a 16th-century manor house

A garden oasis like in a movie: the Arboretum in Trsteno

17 Bota Šare 🍴
⌐ 66 km/41 mi ⌐
18 Viganj 🏄
⌐ 6 km/3.7 mi ⌐
19 Aminess Grand Azur Hotel 🛏

DAY 8
⌐ 9 km/5.6 mi ⌐
🚢
20 Korčula 🏛
⌐ 7 km/4.3 mi ⌐
21 vineyards 🛍
🚢
⌐ 155 km/96 mi ⌐
🚢
22 Hvar 😎
⌐ 77 km/48 mi ⌐

with extravagant gardens. **After another 35 km (22 miles), you simply must stop in** Mali Ston for the fresh oysters at ⑰ **Bota Šare** → p. 96! The route **continues over the Pelješac peninsula → p. 93 on the D414 for 66 km (41 miles) to** ⑱ **Viganj** where crystal clear water and perfect surfing conditions await. You can rent the proper equipment at places such as Water Donkey. Check in for the night at the ⑲ **Aminess Grand Azur Hotel → p. 95, 6 km (4 miles) back on the D414 towards Ston**.

The next morning, it's time to **hop from island to island – the first trip is rather short from Orebić to the island of Korčula → p. 90.** The pleasant little town of ⑳ **Korčula** exudes Mediterranean charm. About **7 km (4 miles) south, via the Lumbarajska ulica, stop in Lumbarda → p. 92** where the vintner Bire produces the best certified organic wines cultivated in his ㉑ **vineyards → p. 92** that are part of his agritourism operation. **Take the ferry from Korčula back to Orebić. Cross back over the Pelješac peninsula using the same route as before for about 70 km (43 miles) to Ston and back to the mainland and then continue on the E65 to the north. In Drvenik, board the ferry to the island of** ㉑ **Hvar → p. 57. On the curvy Road 116 that runs from the ferry harbour Sućuraj for 77 km (48 miles) to the west,** you will drive past aromatic fields of lavender, pretty bathing bays and isolated villages before you reach the glamorous  **Hvar town** → p. 58. Stylish accommodation awaits in the historic **Palace**.

Take the same route **back to the mainland and leave the harbour of Drvenik on the coastal road E 65 to the north.** The beaches lined with palm treets along the ㉔ **Makarska Riviera** → p. 61 will lure you into the Adriatic Sea for a swim against the backdrop of the Biokovo Mountains. At the harbour in **Makarska, board the ferry to Sumartin** to cross over to the island of ㉕ **Brač** → p. 52. From the harbour, follow **the 113 for 15 km (9 miles) inland to Gornji Humac** → **p. 55 and turn left onto the 115 towards Bol** on the south coast. After such a long trip, you've more than earned a relaxing afternoon on the most famous beach in Croatia, the ㉖ **Golden Cape (Zlatni rat)** → p. 52. Plan to spend two nights at the **Bluesun Elaphusa** → p. 55.

The next morning, explore the quieter charms of the island **as you drive to** Pučišća → **p. 56, approx. 20 km (12 miles) on the 115 to the north, and** Škrip → **p. 55, approx. 20 km along the northern coastal road heading west**. Then take the 113 for 30 km (19 miles) back to Bol.

On the last day, explore busy ㉗ **Supetar** → **p. 56, approx. 35 km (22 km) to the north on the 113**, and enjoy the island flair. Then take the **ferry back to the mainland and return to** ㉘ **Split.**

---

2   THE HIDDEN TREASURES OF VIS

START: ❶ Vis	1 day
END: ❶ Vis	Cycling time
Distance: Strenuous	(without stops)
🚲 58 km/36 miles ▮▮▮ Height:	6 hours
1,100 m/3,600 ft	

COSTS: 120 kuna for lunch, boat to the little neighbouring island of ❼ **Ravnik** with its green cave approx. 100 kuna, bike rental approx. 120 kuna

WHAT TO PACK: drinks, swim gear, sun protection

IMPORTANT TIPS: There are several steep ascents and descents on this tour! You can rent a bike at places such as **Vis Special** (Korzo 33 | tel. 098 9 29 08 35 | www.vis-special.com).

Remote bays perfect for swimming, picture-perfect konobas, vineyards, lavender, oleander and crystal-clear water – the island of Vis (apart from its two main towns) is still a largely undiscovered gem. If you're up to it, you can undertake this 60 km (37 mile) tour of the island by bike.

① Vis

10 km/6 mi

② Fabrika

11 km/6.8 mi

③ Titova špilja

2 km/1.2 mi

④ Konoba Pol Murvu

6 km/3.7 mi

09:00am Start off from the town of **① Vis → p. 73**. The first 10 km (6 miles) **on the 117 climb steadily to the west**. Cross through a valley framed by mountain ranges and past the pre-Romanesque church of Sv. Mihovil, which marks the route's highest point at 385 m (1,263 ft). After that, a sometimes **steeply winding road leads down to the sea and Komiža → p. 73**. At this point, you've already more than earned an iced coffee at the café **② Fabrika** (Riva Sv. Mikule). **Then bike 500 m (546 yards) back up-hill on the 117 until the road branches off to the southeast and climbs around Hum, the highest mountain on the island (587 m/1,925 ft). About 7 km (4.3 miles) later, signs in Podšpilje point the way** to Tito's cave. From here, the route to cave entrance heads north for **700 m (765 yards) to the junction at Žena Glava and then another 600 m (656 yards) to the west**. In the hamlet of Borovik, you will spy the steps that lead to **③ Titova špilja (Tito's Cave)**. The partisan leader Josip Broz Tito set up his military headquarters here during the last months of the Second World War. After exploring the cave on your own, **return to the junction and cycle a few metres straight on** before stopping for lunch at **④ Konoba Pol Murvu** (tel. 021 715 117 | Budget–Moderate) in the village of Žena Glava.

01:30pm Head back to the 117 and cycle above the coast towards the east. Near the village of Plisko Polje, 4 km

Honey, it seems we're not the only ones going to Stiniva Bay in a boat!

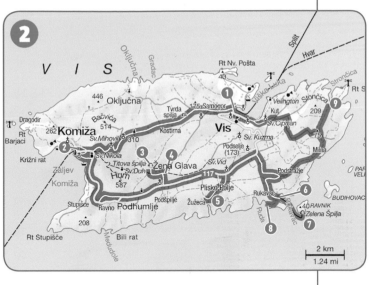

2

(2.5 miles) from Podšpilje, turn towards Marinje Zemlje, 1.5 km (1 mile) further to the southwest, then walk steeply downhill for approx. 20 minutes to ⑤ INSIDER TIP **Uvala Stiniva**, a magical bay secluded behind the rocks with only a narrow gap out to the sea. Enjoy a well-earned break for a swim! **Return to Plisko Polje and follow the main road for 1.5 km (1 mile) to the east and then turn right onto the road that leads downhill to ⑥ Rukavac**. In this small village with its bay ringed by vegetation, embark on a boat trip to ⑦ **Ravnik Island** with its lesser known, but still quite beautiful **Green Cave (Zelena špilja)** that turns turquoise green when the sun shines on it. **Once you're back on Vis,** check out another lovely beach, namely the one on ⑧ **Uvala Srebrna**, the silver bay, **250 m (273 yards) west of Rukavac**.

06:00pm Back in Podstražje village, follow the road along for 5 km (3.1 miles) until a dirt road branches off to the right and follow this track for another 2.5 km (1.5 miles) to ⑨ INSIDER TIP **Stončica Bay**. A footpath leads from the car park down to the sandy beach; snacks and drinks are served at **Konoba Stončica** *(tel. 021 711 669 | Budget)*. A little road meanders along the coast from Stončica for about 9 miles back to ① Vis.

⑤ Uvala Stiniva

7.6 km/4.7 mi

⑥ Rukavac

1.8 km/1.2 mi

⑦ Ravnik Island

2.7 km/1.7 mi

⑧ Uvala Srebrna

7.6 km/4.7 mi

⑨ Stončica Bay

9 km/5.6 mi

① Vis

FROM ZADAR TO NATURAL WONDERS IN THE HINTERLAND

START: ① Zadar
END: ⑨ Šibenik

Distance:
➡ 490 km/304 miles

5 days
Driving time
(without stops)
7 hours

COSTS: aprox. 370 kuna for petrol, approx. 260 kuna for admission fees, approx. 4,500 kuna for food & accommodation

WHAT TO PACK: hiking boats, rain gear, tent, sun protection, swim gear

IMPORTANT: The best time to visit ⑤ Plitvice Lakes National Park is early in the morning before the busloads of tourists arrive!
Make sure to pack provisions for the route to Plitvice – there is hardly anywhere to get food or drink along the way!

A magnificent karst-studded natural landscape, a delightful Mediterranean coast and harbour towns hiding archaeological and architectural gems within their old walls are sure to please – the northern Dalmatian coast packs all the noteworthy aspects of the region into one small area. This route starting in Zadar combines fascinating natural parks with the wonderful coastal towns of Zadar and Šibenik .

DAY 1

① Zadar
〔 21 km/13 mi 〕
② Sv. Križ
〔 52 km/32 mi 〕
③ Starigrad-Paklenica
〔 16 km/10 mi 〕
④ Camp Vrata Velebita

DAY 2
〔 18 km/11 mi 〕
⑤ Paklenica National Park

In ① **Zadar → p. 44**, take time to visit the **Archaeological Museum → p. 45** and the church of **Sv. Donat → p. 46** before **driving north on the 306.** When you get to **Nin** (km 16), go inside the little ancient Croatian church of ② **Sv. Križ**. Then **drive back southeast for 17 km (10.5 miles) to the junction with the E65 and take the Adria Magistrale towards Rijeka. The route over the Maslenica Bridge will bring you to** ③ **Starigrad-Paklenica** in about 36 km (22 miles). This natural park on the coast is a popular tourist destination and a favourite swimming spot. Pitch your tent at ④ **Camp Vrata Velebita** (*Put Ljubotića 50 | Tribanj | tel. 095 9 14 96 29 | vratavelebita.com | Budget*), **approx. 16 km (10 miles) north of Starigrad on the E65**, which is part of an organic agritourism operation.

Early the next morning, **head back to Starigrad to get to the main entrance of the** ⑤ ★ **Paklenica National Park** (*admission varies by season from 40 kuna | tel. 023 36 91 55 | www.paklenica.hr*), a true hiking and climbing paradise. The two canyons, Mala (little) and Velika (big)

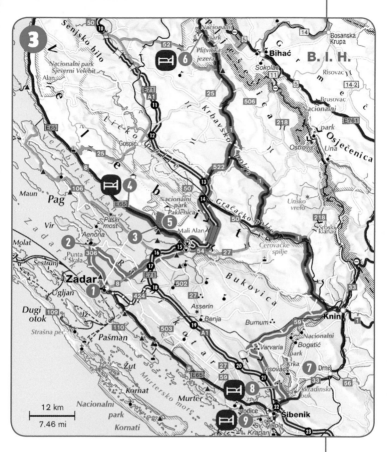

Paklenica, which were carved into the karst by the wild streams of the Velebit mountains, are the heart of this park. The main attraction in both canyons are the free climbers who hang like colourful spiders on the rocky walls. At a height of 400 m (1,312 ft), the wall Anića kuk is considered to be quite the challenge. The routes vary in difficulty from 3 to 8b+. Beginners and parents with small children will find easier climbing routes in the INSIDERTIP *klanci* section – but please make sure that kids wear a helmet! Hike for two hours along the mix of easy and steeply climbing trails through the **Velika Paklenica** canyon, past several mills to the little lodge of **Lugarnica** *(June–Sept, daily 10:30am–4:30pm)*, which serves simple food and

Incomparable waterfalls in the Plitvice Lakes National Park

drinks. **Hike back to the entrance via the same route** and camp for another night at Vrata Velebita.

DAY 3

To get to your next destination, **drive along the E65 back towards the Maslenica Bridge and turn left before the bridge onto the toll road A1 heading to Karlovac and Zagreb. After 48 km (30 miles), take exit 13 (Gornja Ploča).** The national road 1 crosses over the rocky landscape of Karjina via Udbina and Korenica. After driving **50 km (31 miles),** you will be astounded by the lush green vegetation at the main entrance to the 200 km² area of the ⑥ ★ Plitvice Lakes National Park *(spring/autumn daily 8am–6pm, summer daily 7am–8pm, winter daily 9am–*

⑥ Plitvice Lakes
National Park

4pm | July/Aug 180 kuna, April–June, Sept/Oct 110 kuna, Nov–March 55 kuna | tel. 053 75 10 15 | www.np-plitvicka-jezera.hr), which has been a Unesco World Heritage site since 1979. The thickly forested mountains are dotted with valley basins in which waterfalls and streams cascade over the sides, connecting 16 lakes with each other. Paths wind through the magical landscape to highlights such as a 76 m (250 ft) high waterfall. On the round trip route, you will walk for two hours along the upper lakes and then another two hours along the lower ones. Stop for coffee at the bistro **Kozjačka Draga** on Lake Kozjak. Afterwards, rest your head for the night at **Hotel Jezero** *(229 rooms | tel. 053 75 10 15 | Moderate)* near the main entrance to the park.

Follow the same route back on the B1 the next morning, but drive further past Gračac (67 km/42 miles) towards Knin (about another 50 km/31 miles) until you come to the river Krka. A 45-km stretch of the river between Kninsko Polje and Skradin has been declared a conservation area. Drive along the banks or near the river **on the roads 59 (34 km/21 miles) and 56 (16 km/10 miles) to Skradin** in order to access the 111 km² area of the ⑦ ★ **Krka National Park** *(Skradin entrance daily 8am–6pm | Roški slap entrance daily 9am–6pm | 110–200 kuna, price varies by season | tel. 022 20 17 77 | www. npkrka.hr)*. The water of the Krka is high in calcium carbonate and it made the typical karst formations. The lower course of the river here tumbles over cascades into the valley. From the park entrance, take a boat to the 46 m (150 ft) high waterfall **Skradinski buk,,** which is considered to be the highest tuff barrier in Europe. Put on your swimsuit and take a shower under the foaming water. A small **museum** with a simple eatery displays a collection of local customs and traditional dress. **Return to Skradin** where the best place to stay is the mid-range hotel ⑧ **Skradinski buk** *(28 rooms | Burinovac 2 | tel. 022 77 17 71 | www.skradinskibuk.hr | Budget)*.

After breakfast, follow **the D56 to the southeast (9 km/5.6 miles) and the D33 for 11 km (6.8 miles) to the southwest to get back to the sea** and the romantic little town of ⑨ **Šibenik** → p. 39. Its **old town centre** with its unusual Renaissance and Baroque buildings makes for a nice change. The wine bar **Vino i Ino** is an architectural and culinary delight. End the tour with a day at the beach and book an apartment at the **Solaris Beach Resort**.

DAY 4

187 km/116 mi

⑦ Krka National Park

7 km/4.3 mi

⑧ Skradinski buk

DAY 5

20 km/12.5 mi

⑨ Šibenik

A VISIT TO VINEYARDS AND OLIVE GROVES

START: ❶ Split **END:** ⑯ Ston	**4 days** Driving time (without stops) **4 hours**
Distance: ➡ **210 km/130 miles**	

COSTS: petrol 120 kuna, ferry crossings 750 kuna, accommodation/food & drink 3,000 kuna
WHAT TO PACK: swim gear

IMPORTANT TIPS: Decide ahead of time who will be the designated driver and who will taste the wine!
It's best to book a wine tasting, lodging and a cycling tour with the winemaker Mario Bartulović *(tours@bartul.com)* well in advance!
Info about the ferry connections: *www.jadrolinija.hr*

Some of the best Dalmatian wines ripen on the slopes of the island of Korčula → p. 90 and the Pelješac peninsula → p. 93, and excellent olive oil is produced in this region as well. Its not that suprising given that the area has a long tradition of cultivation dating back to when Greek colonists from Siracusa in Sicily planted grapevines and olive trees here more than 3,000 years ago.

DAY 1

❶ Split

79 km/49 mi

❷ Uljara Zlokić

21 km/13 mi

❸ Aminess Lume Hotel

Around 10am, embark on this tour of delights and leave ❶ **Split → p. 65** behind you. **The car ferry 604** run by *Jadrolinija (www.jadrolinija.hr)* only takes three hours for the crossing to Vela Luka on Korčula, which used to be the port of export for the island's wines and oils. The ❷ **Uljara Zlokić** *(Mon–Fri 10am–noon, 6pm–8pm | Ulica 6. br. 13 | tel. 098 9 29 50 73 | www.uljarazlokic.com)* bottles internationally acclaimed olive oils. In an exhibit attached to the oil mill, you can see tools and machinery used in the cultivation of olives. Don't forget to try the Zlokić oils before you leave. Afterwards, drive **10 km (6.2 miles) through olive groves on the 118** heading eastward and **at the junction take the Ulica 1 south for 2 km (1.2 miles) to Blato**. From here, turn to go **towards Prizba on the southern coast**. Enjoy the beautiful vistas as you drive along **the coastal road to the east for 8 km (5 miles) to Brna.** Tiny offshore islands are dotted between deep sheltered bays. Plan to stay the night in Brna and check into the ❸ **Aminess Lume Hotel** *(76 rooms | tel. 052 85 86 00 | www.aminess.com | Moderate)* – a good, quietly situated mid-range hotel.

The tour continues inland on the next day, **heading northeast for 4 km/2.5miles from Brna to Smokvica**, the major winegrowing area for the *Pošip* and *Rukatac* grape varieties that produce light and fresh white wines. At the winery ❹ **Toreta** *(Smokvica 165 | tel. 020 83 21 00)*, you should definitely try the excellent quality wines. The next **17 km (10.5 miles) on the 118 to Pupnat** are quite an adventure! The sometimes dizzying stretch of road meanders above the coast to ❺ **Pupnatska Luka** (11 km/6.8 miles).

DAY 2

5 km/3.1 mi

❹ Toreta

11 km/6.8 mi

❺ Pupnatska Luka

A hearty wine should go well with this: traditional *peka* dish

You simply must go for a swim here in one of the prettiest bays on Korčula. **Drive a few kilometres further and treat yourself to a hearty lunch** in ❻ **Pupnat** at the **Konoba Mate** *(tel. 020 71 71 09 | Moderate)*. Located right next to the church and surrounded by grapevines, enjoy the truly homegrown and homemade food. Bask in the romantic atmosphere of this little town before getting back on the road. After **another 11 km (6.8 miles) on the D118, you will arrive in the picturesque town of** ❼ **Korčula → p. 90** where you should plan to spend the second night.

On the following morning, **hop aboard the ferry to Orebić on Pelješac**. It is a short crossing, but it offers the most beautiful view of Korčula's old town. ❽ **Orebić → p. 94** itself is an old seafaring town, but as soon as you **drive inland along the 414 towards Donja Banda and cross over the hills,** there are vineyards everywhere. As the soil is barren and rocky, the grapevines are planted on small fields

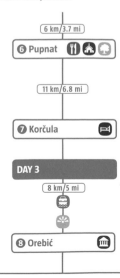

6 km/3.7 mi

❻ Pupnat

11 km/6.8 mi

❼ Korčula

DAY 3

8 km/5 mi

❽ Orebić

16 km/10 mi

9 Bartulović Winery

DAY 4

3 km/1.9 mi

10 Potomje

9 km/5.6 mi

11 Grgić Vina

surrounded by high dry stone walls to protect them from the wind. About **2 km (1.2 miles) after Donja Banda, you will come to the village of Prizdrina** (pop. 20) with its old stone houses. The famous vintner Mario Bartulović will let you look over his shoulder as he works at **9 Bartulović Winery** *(4 rooms, 1 bungalow | tel. 020 74 25 06 | www. vinarijabartulovic.hr | Moderate)*. Using the southern Dalmatian grape variety of *Plavac mali*, he produces the excellent red wines sold under the brand *Bartul*. As Mario himself likes to keep fit, he will take overnight guests along on **INSIDER TIP** *wine tours by mountain bike (from 500 kuna per person | tours@bartul.com)*. Cycle over field paths and through vineyards to the neighbouring wineries to taste the characteristic Pelješac wines.

After spending the night, **drive a few kilometres the next morning on the 414 to the southeast** into the heart of the *Dingač* growing region, the village of **10 Potomje**. Pass through the adventurous and narrow tunnel carved into the rock by the wine makers **to get to the southern coast** where the special grape variety of *Plavac mali* ripens on the steep slopes. The **narrow road snakes along the terraced vineyards to the east for 8 km (5 miles) to Trstenik**. The town is home to the winery of **11 Grgić Vina** *(tel. 020 74 80 90 | www.grgic-vina.com)*, which belongs to the most famous of the Pelješac wine makers, Mike Grgich. He made his fortune and a name for himself in California before returning to his homeland where he began to

Winemakers on the Pelješac peninsula compete to make the best reds

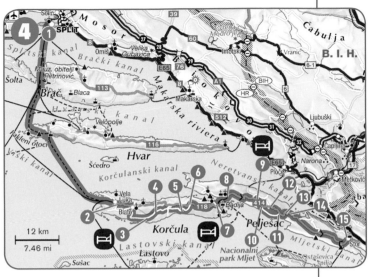

make internationally acclaimed *Dingač* wines. **Cross over the steep mountain ridge for 2 km (1.2 miles) back to the north and then take the 414 for 5 km (3 miles) to the west to get to Pijavičino**. Ivo Skaramuča is hoping to become Pelješac's best vintner with his estate ⑫ **Vina Skaramuča** *(tel. 098 9 12 52 75 | dingac-skaramuca.hr)*. Unlike others, he ages his *Dingač* wines in oak barrels, so it is definitely worth the little detour to his vineyard. **Now head eastwards along the 414 until you come to Janjina (approx. 9 km / 5.5 miles)** and the ⑬ **Taverna Domanoeta** *(Janjina 51 | tel. 020 74 14 06 | Budget)*. The Croatian/Italian couple that owns the taverna do all they can to please every guest. Another **2 km (1.2 mile) on the 414 will bring you to the northern coast near** ⑭ **Drače**. Mussels and oysters are farmed in the very shallow bay. **The final stop on the tour is** ⑮ **Ston → p. 95**, **which lies 30 km (18.6 miles) to the southeast on the 414**. Not only does **Vinarija Miloš** *(Ponikve 15 | tel. 020 75 30 98 | www.milos.hr)* bottle a full-bodied *Plavac Stagnum*, but also it has begun to produce organic olive oil and tea. *Oblica* and *Pastrica* are the names of the autochthonous olive varieties that lend Frano Miloš' oil its fine, fruity note. It even seems to have a taste of the maquis so characteristic of Pelješac.

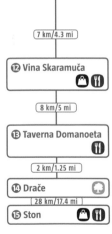

7 km/4.3 mi

⑫ **Vina Skaramuča**

8 km/5 mi

⑬ **Taverna Domanoeta**

2 km/1.25 mi

⑭ **Drače**

28 km/17.4 mi

⑮ **Ston**

SPORTS & ACTIVITIES

The coast of Dalmatia is no longer all about sailing, surfing, diving and snorkelling.

More and more marked hiking and mountain biking trails as well as climbing routes have opened up many new possibilities for an active getaway, particularly during the off season.

CYCLING & MOUNTAIN BIKING

Whether you're into road racing, mountain biking, electric bikes or just riding for pleasure, you can find an appropriate challenge in Dalmatia. Dedicated cycle paths are marked out in many places – some of which run along trails formerly used by shepherds. A few tourist as-

sociations produce cycle maps showing routes and altitude profiles, or make this information available for download (along with GPS data) from their websites. Bike and mountain bike hire is also available in most tourist resorts (including electric bikes). Island hopping is particularly good fun on two wheels: travel from island to island with a motor glider and explore the different attractions and landscapes on an off-road bike.

DIVING & SNORKELLING

Thanks to its many small islands and reefs and an incredibly biodiversity, the Croatian Adriatic is a paradise for divers and snorkellers. You can even see fish, crabs and octopuses when snorkelling

Sporty action or calmness and reflection? In Dalmatia, both poles come together in harmony

from the beach. If you join a guided diving trip then you won't need a diving permit. However solo diving is only permitted with a Diver's Card, which you can obtain from a harbourmaster's office if you present your diving certification (approx. £280/$375 per year). Information: *www.croatia.hr)*.

tained from local tourist information offices, in many holiday villages, at a number of travel agents or online at *ibarstvo.mps.hr.* A day permit costs around £7/$9 and a three-day permit around £17.50/$23, depending on the location and the gear you use.

FISHING

One-day or multi-day permits are required for fishing; these can be ob-

HIKING

The sparsely populated natural landscapes of Dalmatia have the potential to be a genuine paradise for hikers, but sadly in many places there is a lack of properly maintained trails, signs or maps. However the National and Nature Parks, the Biokovo mountains, the island of Mljet, the canyons of Paklenica and Plitvice all offer visitors a wide selection of well-signposted and documented paths. Islands like Hvar and Brač that are popular with tourists are also well mapped out. Information is available from the relevant tourist information offices; however we strongly advise that you stick strictly to the mapped paths, as undiscovered mines left over from the Yugoslavian War pose a very real danger to hikers who head off-track.

RAFTING, CANOEING & SEA KAYAKING

A trip down the Cetina upstream of Omiš is a must for fans of white-water rafting, and can be booked through a number of providers, such as the *Omiš Rafting Association (tel. 021 86 31 61 | www.raft.hr)*. The Krupa and Zrmanja rivers in North Dalmatia are popular with canoeists, and a five-hour trip through the rapids of the Zrmanja down to its mouth in the Adriatic can be booked with the agency *Kornatica (Put Slanice 7 | Murter | tel. 099 2 43 73 23 | www.kornatica.com)*. If you prefer to race down the river in a raft then visit the *Riva Rafting Centar (Obrovac | tel. 023 68 99 20 | www.riva-rafting-centar.hr)* near Zadar. The gentle and environmentally friendly sport of ⚓ *sea kayaking* is particularly enjoyable in the Elaphiti archipelago and the Kornati National Park. You can hire kayaks in any of the larger tourist resorts, or just join a guided tour. On Korčula, for example, this would take you from Lumbarda to the neighbouring islands of Vrnik and Planjak. The provider *Korčula Adventures (Lumbarda 44 | Lumbarda | tel. 098 34 41 82 | www.korcula-adventures.com)* also rents out **INSIDER TIP** glass-bottomed kayaks!

ROCK CLIMBING

Climbing is very popular in Dalmatia, and new areas and routes are being added all the time. The Paklenica National Park is a classic destination on the coast, with rock faces up to 1,600 m/5,250 ft tall and 360 routes ranging in difficulty from 3 to 8b+. The most popular spot is the 400 m/1,310 ft peak of *Anića kuk*. We recommend the multilingual climbing guide "Paklenica" by Boris Čujić, which is available from the National Park authority *(tel. 023 36 91 55 | www.np-paklenica.hr)*. The steep slopes of the Cetina gorge near Omiš boast over 200 routes in 14 different sectors, and

Zlatni rat near Bol on the island of Brač is considered one of Dalmatia's top surfing spots

the newest area, *Perivoj*, has 12 new climbs. Information: *Tourist Info Omiš (tel. 021 86 13 50 | www.tz-omis.hr) and www.climbingomis.com.* Thrill-seekers can also find ten routes in the *Stara kava* climbing area on the island of Dugi otok. Information: *Tourist Info Sali (tel. 023 37 70 94 | www.dugiotok.hr)*

WELLBEING

Most modern hotels feature large spas with saunas and steam rooms, and offer a wide range of treatments that can also be taken advantage of by external visitors. For a spa of truly epic proportions try the hotel *Iadera (tel. 023 50 09 11 | www.falkensteiner.com)* in Petrčane, for example. Guests at the hotel *Korinjak* (see p. 49) on Iž can enjoy meditation and yoga in the intimate setting of a mid-range hotel.

WINDSURFING, SAILING & KITE SURFING

With 1,184 islands and 1,777 km/1,104 miles of coastline, Croatia is a sailing paradise with plenty of idyllic coasts and romantic fishing villages to cast anchor in. The infrastructure for sailors is superb, with fully modernised marinas and harbours. Contact the *Croatian National Tourist Office (UK Tel. +44 208 563 7979 | www.croatia.hr). The Adriatic Croatia International Club (www.aci-club.hr)* maintain a number of marinas in Dalmatia. Wind- and kitesurfers regularly congregate in the following areas: Orebić, where high speeds can be reached in the channel between Korčula and Pelješac when wind conditions are favourable *(www.orebic.hr);* the strait separating Bol on Brač from the island of Hvar *(www.bol.hr);* and Nin to the north of Zadar *(www.surfmania.hr).*

TRAVEL WITH KIDS

Children get a warm welcome, and tourist providers here do their utmost to keep kids entertained.

The numerous beaches and bathing opportunities also provide plenty of variety and fun. Bathing shoes will keep children safe from stones and sea urchins and allow them to devote themselves to exploring everything that makes the Croatian coast such an adventurous place: the cracks and fissures in the rocks, the tiny pools containing crabs and fishes, collecting jetsam and shells – the list goes on! Older children can spend hours exploring the coast with a snorkel and flippers, or can learn to dive and windsurf. And in the unlikely event that boredom sets in then there are plenty of places to visit nearby.

ZADAR REGION

BEAR CUBS (138 C1) (*ω E1*)

In the village of Kuterevo in the Velebit mountains, around 30 km (18.6 miles) from the coast and from Senj, an animal welfare initiative has set up an enclosure for injured, sick or lost young brown bears. The goal is to reintroduce the bears back into the wild once they are old enough. Until then they are kept well in large enclosures where visitors can watch them as they play around, play-fight or nap. The littlest ones are particularly cute. *May–Nov daily 8am– sunset | admission 30 kuna | Velebitsko utočište za mlade medvjede Kuterevo | Pod crikvom 103 | Kuterevo | tel. 053 79 92 22*

Photo: Exploring the Kornati archipelago by boat

Climbing wizards and captains – Croats love children and have lots of fun to offer them

FALCONRY CENTRE (140 B2) *(🗺 G4)*
The falconer Emilio Menđusić takes care of injured birds and releases them back into the wild, and his team at the Falconry Centre also carry out scientific research and run educational programmes – e.g. for school students. Visitors will enjoy a 45-minute tour, which naturally includes a falconry display featuring eagles, hawks and buzzards. The *Sokolarski Centar* lies on the outskirts of the village of Dubrava. *In summer daily 9am–7pm | 45 kuna, children 35 kuna | Škugori |*
Dubrava kod Šibenika | 7 km (4.3 miles) south of Šibenik | tel. 091 5 06 76 10 | sokolarskicentar.com

FUN PARK MIRNOVEC
(139 D5) *(🗺 E4)*
The Wild West, pirate land and outer space all await intrepid adventurers at this pleasure park which opened in 2017 (the first of its kind in Croatia). If you dare to ride the roller coaster and you'll be rewarded with splendid views of the sea from above. Once you pay the park's

admission fee, you can go on as many rides as your stomach will allow you. Take a break from this rough life at sea in the *Fat Pirate Cave* restaurant. *In summer daily 3–11pm | admission 135 kuna, children 108 kuna | Jankolovački put 9 | 3 km/1.9 miles from Biograd na Moru | www.funparkmirnovec.com*

HIGH-ROPE COURSE (138 C4) (*ﾉ E3*)
In Kožino, a few kilometres from Zadar, you can find the *Adventure Park*, a challenging high-rope course in a spruce forest. After a brief induction session, children (and adults) can test their nerve on wobbly bridges, rope ladders and a range of obstacles that will get their adrenalin pumping – all in perfect safety, of course. *In summer daily 10am–6pm | 100 kuna | Kožino | www.adventure-park.com*

Ok I admit it's nice in Paklenica Park, but tomorrow it's the beach again!

PHOTO SAFARI ON THE VELEBIT (139 D3–4) (*ﾉ E3*)
Speed by jeep through the Paklenica National Park, stopping on the way for photos of the picturesque Winnetou filming locations and with a bit of luck, you may even spot a few wild horses: this mountainous landscape impresses both old and young alike. Day excursions are organised by *Hotel & Travel Agency Rajna (Franje Tuđmana 105 | 490 kuna (from 4 people, otherwise 20 percent surcharge) for a guided day trip, incl. admission and food | Franje Tuđmana 105 | Starigrad-Paklenica | tel. 098 27 28 78 | www.hotel-rajna.com/english/fotosafari)*

SANDY BEACHES NEAR NIN AND ZATON (138 C4) (*ﾉ E3*)
There are few places on the Dalmatian coast where small children can safely play in the sand, build castles and splash around in the water, but the shallow fine-shingle and sand beaches on the lagoon of Nin and Zaton are ideal for toddlers.

INSIDER TIP▸ SOLARIS AQUAPARK (139 E6) (*ﾉ F4*)
An aquatic adventure playground in the Solaris Beach Resort complex near Šibenik. Toddlers will especially love the *kiddy world*. *Mid-April–Oct daily 9am–8pm (depending on the weather) | 110 kuna, children 90–120 cm 80 kuna | www.solaris.hr*

SPLIT REGION

BATHING ON A FAMILY-FRIENDLY BEACH (141 D4) (*ﾉ J5*)
The pebble beach of *Dugi rat* in *Brela* shelves so gently that even very small children can splash around safely in the water. The pebbles are small and a lot more pleasant than the sharp stones of

the rocky beaches. A small pine forest provides shade and there are several cafés serving child-friendly snacks.

BOTANICAL GARDEN (141 E4) (*ω J6*)

Hundreds of native plant species flourish on the edge of Biokovo Nature Park in the 16.5 hectare Kotišina Botanical Gardens; stone plaques bear the names of the individual species. *Free admission | 3 km (1.9 mile) north of Makarska*

PLAYING CAPTAIN

Drifting along on one of the replica historical sailboats through Croatia's islands, helping to hoist the anchor, bathing in remote bays, throwing out the anchor in front of "pirate nests" and jumping into crystal-clear waters straight from the boat: all of these things are fun for children. The fact that they will walk along fortress walls, stroll around historic towns and splash about in the water on family-friendly beaches just adds to their enjoyment. Local tourist information offices will provide information about day and mini cruises.

Don't scare it away: a "crane" at Šipanska Luka

DUBROVNIK REGION

CROATIA DIVERS (141 D5) (*ω H7*)

Children only have to be eight years old to be welcome in the kids' programme of the diving school. Bobby and Marjolein will take eight to ten-year-olds on the two-hour *PADI Bubblemaker (around 350 kuna)* taster session, during which the children will dive with a mask and a bottle for 30 minutes. Children of ten and over can also participate in the junior programme, which will allow them to obtain the *Padi junior Open Water Diver* certificate. *Obala 1 | Vela Luka | Korčula | tel. 091 2 56 78 04 | www.croatiadivers.com*

ISLAND HOPPING FROM GRUŽ (143 D5) (*ω L7*)

Had enough of beach shoes and stony beaches? Then take a ● boat trip to the island of *Lopud* from Dubrovnik's harbour, Gruž. Go for a short walk in Lopud through the wild maquis to reach the beach, where you will finally be able to build some sandcastles. If you like, you can take the ferry further to Koločep and Šipan. But make sure not to miss the last boat back. The timetable is available at *www.jadrolinja.hr*

LIBERAN SURFCENTER (142 A4) (*ω J7*)

The channel dividing Pelješac and Korčula is an ideal place to learn to windsurf. Children under 13 can take part in a four-day course at the windsurf centre in Viganj, near Orebić, which involves four hours of lessons per day. *Children's course around 600 kuna | Ponta | Viganj | liberansurf.eu*

FESTIVALS & EVENTS

There are plenty of festive occasions beyond the major festivals and religious holidays all over Dalmatia – every village has its own holiday to celebrate anchovies, cherries, olive gathering and grape harvests. Simply join in the celebrations – you will be welcomed warmly wherever you go!

EVENTS & FESTIVALS

FEBRUARY

St Blaise's Day (Sv. Vlaho) on February 3rd is celebrated in Dubrovnik with processions, concerts and dancing

MARCH–MAY

Good Friday: Korčula's religious orders tour the old town in a celebratory nighttime *procession*

INSIDER TIP *International Climbers Meeting*: The highlight of this meeting of rock climbers held at the end of April/start of May in the Paklenica gorge is the Big Wall Speed Climbing competition, which makes a fascinating spectacle – even for non-climbers.

Croatia Boat Show: This exhibition in Split is a gathering point for admirers of modern and elegant boats. *croatiaboat show.com*

END OF JUNE/BEGINNING OF JULY

International Children's Festival: during the last week of June and the first of July, Šibenik belongs to the children, with theatre, cinema and lots of fun to participate in. *www.mdf-sibenik.com*

JULY/AUGUST

★ *Dubrovnik Summer Festival:* Six weeks of cultural events in Dubrovnik's Old Town. The programme ranges from klapa choirs, jazz and opera to theatre – from avant-garde to classic

● *Klapa Festival:* The best choirs in Croatia compete at this prestigious festival in Omiš during July. *fdk.hr/festival*

Moreška: The inhabitants of Korčula commemorate the victory of the Christians over the Islamic Moors during the Spanish Reconquista with jousting tournaments and a traditional sword dance

Ultra: Every summer, Split shakes to the sounds of Europe's most famous electronic music festival. Held at the start of July. *ultraeurope.com*

Soundwave: Reggae and hip-hop have never sounded so good than at this amazing beach setting in Tisno on the island of Murter. Held at the end of July. *www.soundwavecroatia.com*

Swordfights, singing and processions – history and tradition are reflected in Dalmatia's festivals

⭐ *Music evenings in Sv. Donat:* Zadar's pre-romanesque church as an antmospheric stage for classical music from various eras. July–mid-August

INSIDER**TIP** *Regius*: Šibenik hosts this two-day alternative music festival. *regi us-festival.com*

Splitsko ljeto (Split Summer): drama, ballet and opera on open-air stages in the old town. *www.splitsko-ljeto.hr*

Saljske Užance: in Sali on Dugi otok the donkeys are let loose to race. Wine, food and music accompany this event. 1st week in August

Summer carnival: A number of traditional carnivals take place in various locations on the Dalmatian coast and islands. The most colourful celebrations are the parades on the Makarska Riviera

Sinjska alka: With a folkloristic festival of chivalry in magnificent uniforms, the event in Sinj commemorates the Croatian victory over the Turks in 1715. A three-day festival on the 1st weekend in August. *www.alka.hr*

SEPTEMBER

Latinsko idro: Murter brings the traditional Adriatic boats back to life; the highlight of the festivities is the regatta at the end of September. *www.latinskoidro.hr*

NATIONAL HOLIDAYS

1 Jan	New Year's Day
6 Jan	Epiphany
March/April	Easter
1 May	Labour Day
May/June	Corpus Christi
22 June	Anti-fascist struggle day
25 June	Statehood Day
5 Aug	Victory Day
15 Aug	Assumption
8 Oct	Independence Day
1 Nov	All Saints' Day
25/26 Dec	Christmas

LINKS, BLOGS, APPS & MORE

www.crobeaches.com Are you looking for the most beautiful, romantic, family-friendly or sandy beach? This website helps you find your ideal beach by performing searches under almost any criteria you can think of

www.instagram.com/domagojsever Fantastic travel photography of the Croatian coast can be found on Instagram, for instance by the freelance photographer Domagoj Sever or the Canadian-Croatian couple Frank and Vera at *franka boutcroatia.* Photos specifically of Dalmatia are posted at *secretdalmatia* and *go.dubrovnik.* There are also some eccentric photos such as on *vrata_splita,* where father and daughter post photos of doors taken in Split

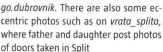

www.hr.undp.org/content/croatia/en/home This English-language UN website provides information about development and environmental programmes implemented on the Croatian coast with the support of the UN

www.chasingthedonkey.com This website is full of great culinary travel tips for Croatia and the Balkan region – including traditional recipes for you to try back home. It also contains a language guide and other amusing facts

secretdalmatia.wordpress.com Interesting blogs on Dalmatia's gastronomy, culture and sights, with good photos and links

www.dalmatianet.com Information on Dalmatian destinations, attractions, accommodation and more

www.expat-blog.com/en/directory/europe/croatia/ Would you like to work, live, move to Croatia? Or just to find out how is life in Croatia? Expats report on their experiences

www.adventurouskate.com/tag/croatia/ Kate travels around the world and blogs engagingly about her adventures – including in Croatia

Regardless of whether you are still researching your trip or already in Dalmatia: these addresses will provide you with more information, videos and networks to make your holiday even more enjoyable.

gohvar.wordpress.com Everything you ever wanted to know about Hvar – from *klapa* choirs to VIP yachts

www.mdc.hr Lists a large selection of Croatian museums with information on collections, contact details and opening times

www.crovideos.com From the simple holiday movie to informative documentaries on customs and music – this site is also home to numerous videos about Dalmatia. There are also Croatian hits in MP3 format to download

www.about-croatia.com/croatian-videos/ Wide collection of videos on Croatia broken down by category (coast, islands, interior...)

www.travelpod.com/travel-blog-country/Croatia/tpod.html Good photos along with numerous videos and blogs in English

HotelRadar Are you looking for the nearest hotels in Dubrovnik or Zadar? No problem with this little app, assessment and booking included

Secret Zadar There's an increasing number of apps about travel destinations in Dalmatia, by private providers as well as by tourist associations. This is one of the more unusual ones, offering little snippets of the history of the region

Makarska Riviera Beaches The most beautiful beaches of the Makarska Riviera including many pictures and info on the quality of the beach, its child-friendliness, sports on offer etc.

Croatia Traffic & Weather Weather, traffic jams, police radar, ferry connections and stuff for sailors: This app, which is available on the website of the breakdown service *HAK (www.hak.hr/en),* contains many useful things for a trip to Croatia

Croatia offline city guide inicall.com offers this app containing everything you need to know about Croatia's sights, also showing hotels, restaurants and nightclubs as well as the best routes by car and on foot – and all of it offline as well

TRAVEL TIPS

ARRIVAL

There is no continuous motorway connection to southern Dalmatia yet. The fastest eastern route runs via Ljubljana and Novo Mesto/Slovenia to Karlovac/Croatia and via Zadar to Split. The western route goes through Trieste/Italy, Koper/Slovenia and Rijeka to the coast. At the moment, the coastal motorway A1 ends in Ploče (information about the current situation: *www.hac.hr*). Slovenian and Croatian motorways are toll roads.

EuroCity trains to Zagreb depart from Germany and Austria. Some trains have through coaches to Rijeka during the summer months, national trains run to Zadar, Šibenik and Split.

There are coaches to Zagreb, Rijeka and Split departing from many major towns. From there you can find connections to Croatia's very well developed public bus network. *www.eurolines.com, www.croatiabus.hr*

Scheduled flights with, for example, Croatia Airlines *(www.croatiaairlines.hr)* go direct to and from Dubrovnik and Split from London Heathrow and Gatwick. A number of Europe's discount carriers serve Croatia, e.g. Ryanair flies to Rijeka from London Stansted and to Zadar from Stansted and Dublin, Easyjet to Dubrovnik from Stansted and Dublin. Inland flights are available from Zagreb to Zadar, Split and Dubrovnik; in summer, there are direct charter flights to Zadar, Split and Dubrovnik.

An attractive alternative to taking the coastal road to southern Dalmatia which has, in some parts, not yet been developed into a motorway is taking the car ferry from Italy: Bari – Dubrovnik (up to 6 times a week), Ancona – Split (daily) or – Stari Grad/Hvar (once a week, July/August twice a week) and – Zadar (daily) are the main routes served by Jadrolinija *(www.jadrolinija.hr)*, SNAV *(www.snav.it)* or Blueline *(www.blueline-ferries.com)*.

RESPONSIBLE TRAVEL

It doesn't take a lot to be environmentally friendly whilst travelling. Don't just think about your carbon footprint whilst flying to and from your holiday destination but also about how you can protect nature and culture abroad. As a tourist it is especially important to respect nature, look out for local products, cycle instead of driving, save water and much more. If you would like to find out more about eco-tourism please visit: *www.ecotourism.org*

BANKS

Banks are usually open *Mon–Fri 7am–7pm, Sat 7am–1pm*. You will find ATMs in the major towns, where you can take money out with debit and credit cards.

BUSES

One alternative for excursions without parking problems is to use the good

From arrival to weather

bus network, which also covers smaller towns along the coast and on the islands. Buses are frequent, comfortable and inexpensive. Timetables at *www.croatiabus.hr*. The journey from Split to Dubrovnik costs 123 kuna for example.

CAMPING

Camping and caravanning are not allowed outside of designated sites. Most of Croatia's campsites – there are more than 520 – are on the Adriatic coast. Croatia has modernized most of its sites to conform to enhanced international standards with many extras such as mini clubs, aqua parks, a wide array of sporting activities and restaurants as well as nightclubs. In some places you can also rent apartments and bungalows. If large sites with more than a thousand pitches are not your thing, you will also find smaller ones. Naturists will appreciate the high standards in the naturist camps. A list and descriptions of the campsites can be found at *www.camping.hr*.

CAR HIRE

International and local car rental places can be found in every sizeable holiday resort. The requirements for renting a vehicle are not the same everywhere. In most cases you need to be at least 21 and have had two years' driving experience. A medium-sized vehicle will cost around 230 kuna a day.

CUSTOMS

In the EU, goods for personal consumption can be imported and exported for free, the following guidelines apply: 800 cigarettes and 10 l spirits. An unlimited volume of wine for private consumption can be brought over the borders of EU countries tax free. You should declare any items at the border which are of more value than your standard travel luggage (including cameras or laptops) as well as cash amounts over 10,000 euros.

CURRENCY CONVERTER

£	HRK	HRK	£
1	8.43	1	0.12
3	25.29	3	0.36
5	42.15	5	0.59
13	110	13	1.54
40	337	40	4.74
75	632	75	8.90
120	1,012	120	14.23
250	2,108	250	29.65
500	4,216	500	59.30

$	HRK	HRK	$
1	6.34	1	0.16
3	19	3	0.47
5	32	5	0.79
13	82	13	2.05
40	254	40	6.31
75	475	75	11.83
120	760	120	18.92
250	1,585	250	39.43
500	3,170	500	78.85

For current exchange rates see www.xe.com

..fee	£1.30/$1.75– £1.75/$2.30 *in a café on the Riva for one espresso*
Ice cream	£1.75/$2.30 *for two scoops*
Snacks	£1.30/$1.75 *for a piece of burek (dumpling with a filling)*
Pizza	£5.25/$7– £8/$10.50 *in a restaurant*
Fuel	£1.29/$1.63 *for 1 l of four-star petrol*
Deck chair	£3.50/$4.66– £5.26/$7 *rent per day*

DRINKING WATER

Tap water is drinkable almost everywhere in Dalmatia, but it is often heavily chlorinated. Since the mineral water in PET bottles is tastier and also inexpensive, it is better to choose that option instead.

DRIVING

National registration and a national driving licence are enough. National registration and a national driving licence are enough for entry. Although it is obligatory in Bosnia and Herzegovina to carry a green insurance card with you, it isn't in Croatia; if you should cross BiH territory on your way to Dubrovnik, you are obliged to show the green card.

Speed limits: 50 km/h (30 mph) in towns, 90 km/h (55 mph) outside towns, 110 km/h (70 mph) on expressways and 130 km/h (80 mph) on motorways. Towing vehicles outside towns 80 km/h (50 mph). The legal alcohol limit is 50 mg per 100 ml. During the winter months (last Sunday in October until last Sunday in March) you must switch on your headlights (dipped) during the day too. School buses must not be overtaken when children are getting in and out. Any crash (a high-visibility jacket is mandatory) has to be reported to the police, who will issue confirmation of the damage; this will avoid potential problems on leaving Croatia. Croatia has a well-developed network of petrol stations; all types of fuel are available in sufficient quantity at EU quality. Croatian motorways are toll roads. The Croatian breakdown service HAK is staffed around the clock: *tel. 1987*. It also runs an app: *Croatia-traffic-info.*

EMBASSIES

US EMBASSY
Ulica Thomasa Jeffersona 2 | Zagreb | tel. 385 1 661 2200 | www.usembassy.gov/croatia

UK EMBASSY
Ivana Lučića 4 | Zagreb | tel. 385 (1) 6009 100 | www.gov.uk/world/organisations/british-embassy-zagreb

CANADIAN EMBASSY
Prilaz Gjure Dezelica 4 | Zagreb | tel. 385 1 488 1200 | croatia.gc.ca

AUSTRALIAN EMBASSY
Centar Kaptol, 3rd floor Nova Ves 11 | Zagreb | tel. 01 4891 200 | www.croatia.embassy.gov.au

EMERGENCY NUMBERS

In an emergency dial the free number 112 where you can also reach English-speaking contacts.

IMMIGRATION

For a maximum stay of 90 days EU (and US) citizens will need an ID card or passport that is valid for the duration of their stay. The same is true for people who travel through Bosnia Herzegovina near Neum on the coastal road to southern Dalmatia. Here, you leave Croatia with all passport and customs checks that apply at the outer borders of the EU before re-entering the country after driving 5 km/3.1 miles through Bosnian territory. Childrens' passports should have a photograph.

FERRIES

The regional ferry connections from the mainland to the islands are largely operated by the vessels of the national shipping company *Jadrolinija (www.jadrolinija.hr)* which runs connections on fast catamarans (passengers only) as well as on car ferries. It is not possible to reserve seats on regional services. For that reason drivers should queue up well before the ship's departure, in peak season two to three hours depending on the route. Timetables and fares are listed on the website. As the routes change every year, the ferry routes shown on the maps are not binding; please obtain local information on the latest developments.

HEALTH

There are no special health risks in Dalmatia. It is important to take good precautions against the sun. Bring a cooling gel to treat sunburns and mosquito bites as well as beach shoes to provide protection against sharp rocks and sea urchins. Hikers visiting the islands should take proper boots that have a good ankle support. A higher boot is also because of the many snakes, s which are venomous.

On the mainland and the larger islan there are pharmacies as well as doctors who speak English. Addresses are available from your accommodation, the local offices of your tour operator and from the tourist information offices.

It is advisable to take out private travel insurance, to include emergency repatriation.

INFORMATION AT YOUR DESTINATION

National information offices can be found in every major town. They are usually called *Tourist Info* or *Turistička zajednica*, abbreviated to *tz.* You will get leaflets, bus and ferry timetables and maps here. In most cases you will also be able to change money. During the peak season the offices are opened daily without a lunch break, while during the low season they are often only open in the morning or they have a longer lunch break. In addition to the national offices, there is a large number of private travel agencies often calling themselves *Tourist-Biro* or something similar; they are specialized in selling private rooms and apartments as well as excursions.

The addresses and websites of all of the tourism offices can be found at *www.croatia.hr* under the relevant destinations.

INFORMATION BEFORE YOUR DEPARTURE

CROATIAN NATIONAL TOURIST OFFICE
– *Lanchesters 162–164 Fulham Palace Road, 2 | W6 9ER London | tel. +44 208 563 7979 | info@croatia-london.co.uk*
– *350 Fifth Avenue, Suite 4003 | 10118*

MONEY & PRICES

Croatia's currency is the kuna. One kuna equals a hundred lipas. Relative to Croatian wages prices are quite high. That is why many locals cannot afford to eat in a good restaurant. Groceries are also quite expensive. As a result, Croatia is no longer a cheap destination for holiday-makers. However, in comparison to other southern European countries you still get good value for money. In tourist centres like Dubrovnik or Hvar, prices for accomodation and food are significantly above the average price level along the coast.

OPENING TIMES

Most restaurants are open continuously from noon until the evening during the main season from April/May to the end of September. Only very few gourmet restaurants can afford restricted opening times or even an off-day. During the low season only some of the hotels, restaurants and shops are open in the holiday resorts. The same is true for museums, whose opening times often change even during a season. It is best to enquire on the spot in the relevant tourist information office.

PHONES & MOBILE PHONES

You'll pay the highest prices making calls from your hotel room; it is cheap-

WEATHER IN SPLIT

	Jan	Feb	March	April	May	June	July	Aug	Sept	Oct	Nov	Dec
Daytime temperatures in °C/°F	10/50	11/52	14/57	18/64	22/72	27/81	31/88	31/88	26/79	21/70	16/61	11/52
Nighttime temperatures in °C/°F	5/41	5/41	7/45	10/50	14/57	18/64	21/70	20/68	17/63	14/57	11/52	6/43
☀ Sunshine hours/day	4	5	6	7	9	10	12	11	8	6	4	3
☂ Precipitation days/month	9	8	8	7	7	6	4	3	6	8	11	12
≈ Water temperature in °C/°F	13/55	12/54	13/55	14/57	17/63	21/70	23/73	24/75	22/72	19/66	16/61	14/57

est to use a phone card and make calls from a payphone. Like everywhere else, though, these are getting scarce due to the widespread use of mobile phones. You can buy phone cards at kiosks, petrol stations and many shops.

The international dialling code for Croatia is 00385; Britain: 0044; North America: 001.

Roaming fees are no longer charged within the EU (since June 2017). However the flat rates which apply in your home country may not be automatically valid in Croatia. Depending on your own domestic rates, you can use a certain volume of data while abroad. If you plan on using your mobile phone often when on holiday, it is advisable to purchase a Croatian pre-paid card.

POST

The opening times of the post offices *(pošta)* are not the same everywhere, but they are usually open *Mon–Fri 7am–7pm, Sat 8am–1pm.* The cost of sending a postcard to another country is 4.60 kuna.

SMOKING

Smoking is not allowed in any public building, restaurant or hotel in Dalmatia. Anyone disregarding this can expect to pay stiff fines.

TIPPING

Good service in a restaurant should be rewarded with around 10 to 15 percent of the bill. The time-tested rule for hotels is to sweeten the employees' job a little with an appropriate tip shortly after you arrive as you will benefit by receiving their attention during your stay.

WHEN TO GO

The peak season with the highest prices in the hotels and restaurants lasts from July to August. During this time it is highly advisable to book your accommodation in advance. In addition prices are often inflated for individual travellers. It is safer and often significantly cheaper to book the same thing in advance through a travel agent. The first two weeks of August are particularly busy because many Italians traditionally spend their holiday in Dalmatia until *Ferragosto* (15 Aug).

The summers tend to be sunny and warm during the day, while the nights are refreshingly cooler. From time to time black clouds build up that turn into thundershowers in the afternoon. Since the Adriatic is not particularly deep, the sea quickly warms up to 20°C / 68°F in the early summer, while temperatures of 26°C / 79°F and higher are measured in August.

The best time to go is mid-May to the end of June, when the gorse is flowering, and September, when the summer heat is not so intense anymore but the Adriatic is still pleasantly warm. During the late summer and autumn months, the cold katabatic bora wind can bring changes in the weather and choppy seas.

WIFI

WiFi access is available in the public spaces of most larger towns, often at the main square, sometimes in the entire old town. In addition most of the *ACI (www.aci-club.hr)* marinas, almost all hotels, hostels and guesthouses have WiFi access.

USEFUL PHRASES CROATIAN

PRONUNCIATION

Here are some hints on how to pronounce Croatian:

č	"ch" as in "church"
š	"sh" as in "shop"
ć	something between "ch" and "tya"
ž	like the "s" in "pleasure"

All vowels are open and should always be pronounced clearly. In combinations of vowels, each vowel is pronounced separately: reuma = re-oo-ma.
When "r" forms a syllable, it must also be pronounced clearly: vrba, Krk.

In words of two syllables, the first syllable is stressed. In words of several syllables, we have marked the syllable that is stressed with a dot.

Abbreviations: coll. = colloquial; f = female speaker

IN BRIEF

Yes/No/Maybe	Da/Ne/Možda
Please/Thank you	Molim/Hvala
Excuse me, please	Oprostite molim/Oprostite molim vas
May I...?/Pardon?	Smijem li...?/Molim?
I would like to.../Have you got ...?	Htio (Htjela f) bih.../Imate li...?
How much is...	Koliko košta...?
I (don't) like that/good/bad	To mi se (ne) dopada/dobro/loše
broken/doesn't work	pokvaren/ne funkcionira
too much/much/little/all/nothing	previše/puno/malo/sve/ništa
Help!/Attention!/Caution!	Pomoć!/Upozorenje!/Oprez!
ambulance/police/fire brigade	vozilo za hitnu pomoć/policija/vatrogasci
Prohibition/forbidden/ danger/dangerous	zabrana/zabranjeno/ opasnost/opasno

GREETINGS, FAREWELL

Good morning!/afternoon!	Dobro jutro/dobar dan!
Good evening!/night!	Dobar večer/laku noć
Hello!/Goodbye!/See you	Zdravo! (halo, bok)/Do vidjenja/Bok! (Čao!)
My name is...	Moje ime je...

Govoriš li hrvatski?

"Do you speak Croatian?" This guide will help you to say the basic words and phrases in Croatian.

What's your name?	Kako se vi zovete? (Kako Vam je ime?) Kako se ti zoveš?
I'm from...	Dolazim iz...

DATE & TIME

Monday/Tuesday/Wednesday	ponedjeljak/utorak/srijeda
Thursday/Friday/Saturday	četvrtak/petak/subota
working day/Sunday/holiday	radni dan/nedjelja/praznik
today/tomorrow/yesterday	danas/sutra/jučer
hour/minute	sat/minuta
day/night/week/month/year	dan/noć/tjedan/mjesec/godina
What time is it?	Koliko je sati?
It's three o'clock/It's half past three	Sad je tri sata/Sad je pola četiri

TRAVEL

open/closed	otvoreno/zatvoreno
entrance/vehicle entrance/ exit/vehicle exit	ulaz/prolaz/ izlaz/prolaz
departure/departure (plane)/arrival	odlazak/odletište/doletište
toilets/ladies/gentlemen	toalet/ženski/muški
(no) drinking water	(ne) pitka voda
Where is...?/Where are...?	Gdje je...?/Gdje su...?
left/right/straight ahead/back	ljevo/desno/ravno/natrag
close/far	blizu/daleko
bus/tram/taxi/stop	autobus/tramvaj/taxi (taksi)/stajaliste
parking lot/parking garage	parkiralište/podzemna garaža
street map/map	plan grada/zemljopisna karta
train station/harbour/airport	željeznička stanica/luka/zračna luka
schedule/ticket/supplement	plan vožnje/vozna karta/doplatak
single/return	jednosmjerno/tamo i natrag
train/track/platform	vlak/peron/željeznički peron
I would like to rent...	Želim unajmiti...
a car/a bicycle/a boat	jedan auto/jedan bicikl/jedan brodić
petrol/gas station / petrol (gas)/diesel	pumpna stanica / benzin/dizel
breakdown/repair shop	nezgoda/radionica

FOOD & DRINK

Could you please book a table for tonight for four?	Molim rezervirajte nam za večeras jedan stol za četiri osobe.

on the terrace/by the window	na terasi/uz prozor
The menu, please	Molim donesite jelovnik.
Could I please have...?	Mogul i dobiti...?
bottle/carafe/glass	flašu/karafu/čašu
knife/fork/spoon	nož/vilicu/žlicu
salt/pepper/sugar/vinegar/oil	sol/papar/šećer/ocat/ulje
milk/cream/lemon	mljeko/vrhnje/citronu
cold/too salty/not cooked	hladno/presoljeno/nedopečeno
with/without ice/sparkling	sa/bez mjehurića (plina)
vegetarian/allergy	vegetarijanac(ci)/alergičar(i)
May I have the bill, please?	Želim platiti, molim
bill/tip	račun/napojnica

SHOPPING

Where can I find...?	Gdje mogu naći ...?
I'd like.../I'm looking for...	Želim.../Tražim...
Do you put photos onto CD?	Možete li spržiti fotografije na CD?
pharmacy/chemist/baker/market	apoteka/drogerija/pekarnica/plac
shopping centre/department store	kupovni centar/robna kuća
food shop/supermarket	trgovina sa namirnicama/supermarket
photographic items/	fotoartikli/
newspaper shop/kiosk	novinarnica/kiosk
100 grammes/1 kilo	sto grama/jedan kilo
expensive/cheap/price/more/less	skupo/jeftino/cijena/manje/više
organically grown	sa biloškog polja

ACCOMMODATION

I have booked a room	Imam jednu sobu rezerviranu.
	(Rezervirao (rezervirala) sam sobu)
Do you have any... left?	Imate li još...
single room/double room	jednokrevetnu sobu/dvokrevetnu sobu
breakfast/half board/full board (American plan)	doručak/polupansion/ puni pansion
at the front/seafront/lakefront	prema naprijed/prema moru/prema jezeru
shower/sit-down bath/balcony/terrace	tuš/kadu/balkon/terasu
key/room card	ključ/karticu za sobu
luggage/suitcase/bag	prtljagu/kofer/tašnu

BANKS, MONEY & CREDIT CARDS

bank/ATM/pin code	banka/bankomat/broj pina
I'd like to change...	Želim promijeniti...
cash/credit card	gotovina/ec kartica/kreditna kartica
bill/coin/change	papirni novac/kovanice/povratni novac

HEALTH

doctor/dentist/paediatrician	lječnik/zubar/dječji lječnik
hospital/emergency clinic	bolnica/hitna služba
fever/pain/inflamed/injured	temperatura/bolovi/upala/povreda
diarrhoea/nausea/sunburn	proljev/povračanje/sunčane opekotine
plaster/bandage/ointment/cream	flaster/zavoj/mast/krema
pain reliever/tablet/suppository	sredstvo protiv bolova/tablete/čepić

POST, TELECOMMUNICATIONS & MEDIA

stamp	marka za pismo
I'm looking for a prepaid card for my mobile	Trebam pokretnu/prepaid karticu za moj mobilni telefon
Where can I find internet access?	Gdje mogui naći internet kafe?
Do I need a special area code?	Trebam li posebni pozivni broj?
dial/connection/engaged	birati/spojeno/zauzeto
socket/adapter/charger	utičnica/adapter-prilagođač/punjač
computer/battery/rechargeable battery	kompjuter/baterija/akumulator
internet address (URL)/e-mail address	adresa na internetu/E-mail adresa
internet connection/wifi	internet priključak/WELAN
e-mail/file/print	E-mail poštu ispisati

LEISURE, SPORTS & BEACH

beach/sunshade/lounger	kupalište/suncobran/ležaljka
low tide/high tide/current	oseka/plima/struja
cable car/chair lift	uspinjaća/lift
(rescue) hut/avalanche	(zaštita) sklonište/lavina

NUMBERS

0	nula	14	četrnaest
1	jedan	15	petraest
2	dva	16	šesnaest
3	tri	17	sedamnaest
4	četiri	18	osamnaes
5	pet	19	devetnaest
6	šest	70	sedamdeset
7	sedam	90	devedeset
8	osam	100	sto
9	devet	200	dvjesto
10	deset	1000	tisuću
11	jedanaest	2000	dvije tisuće
12	dvanaest	½	jedna polovina (pola)
13	trinaes	¼	jedna četrtina (četvrt)

ROAD ATLAS

The green line indicates the Discovery Tour "Dalmatia at a glance"
The blue line indicates the other Discovery Tours

All tours are also marked on the pull-out map

Photo: On the Makarska Riviera

Exploring Dalmatia

The map on the back cover shows how the area has been sub-divided

KEY TO ROAD ATLAS

Autobahn mit Anschlussstellen Motorway with junctions	✱ *Wartenstein* ✱ *Umfallfälle*	Sehenswert: Kultur - Natur Of interest: culture - nature
Autobahn in Bau Motorway under construction		Badestrand Bathing beach
Mautstelle Toll station		Nationalpark, Naturpark National park, nature park
Raststätte mit Übernachtung Roadside restaurant and hotel		Sperrgebiet Prohibited area
Raststätte Roadside restaurant		Kirche Church
Tankstelle Filling-station		Kloster Monastery
Autobahnähnliche Schnell- straße mit Anschlussstelle Dual carriage-way with motorway characteristics with junction		Schloss, Burg Palace, castle
		Moschee Mosque
Fernverkehrsstraße Trunk road		Ruinen Ruins
Durchgangsstraße Thoroughfare		Leuchtturm Lighthouse
Wichtige Hauptstraße Important main road		Turm Tower
Hauptstraße Main road		Höhle Cave
Nebenstraße Secondary road		Ausgrabungsstätte Archaeological excavation
Eisenbahn Railway		Jugendherberge Youth hostel
Autozug-Terminal Car-loading terminal		Allein stehendes Hotel Isolated hotel
Zahnradbahn Mountain railway		Berghütte Refuge
Kabinenschwebebahn Aerial cableway		Campingplatz Camping site
Eisenbahnfähre Railway ferry		Flughafen Airport
Autofähre Car ferry		Regionalflughafen Regional airport
Schifffahrtslinie Shipping route		Flugplatz Airfield
Landschaftlich besonders schöne Strecke Route with beautiful scenery		Staatsgrenze National boundary
		Verwaltungsgrenze Administrative boundary
Alleenstr. Touristenstraße Tourist route		Grenzkontrollstelle Check-point
XI-V Wintersperre Closure in winter		Grenzkontrollstelle mit Beschränkung Check-point with restrictions
Straße für Kfz gesperrt Road closed to motor traffic	**ROMA**	Hauptstadt Capital
8% Bedeutende Steigungen Important gradients	**VENEZIA**	Verwaltungssitz Seat of the administration
Für Wohnwagen nicht empfehlenswert Not recommended for caravans		MARCO POLO Erlebnistour 1 MARCO POLO Discovery Tour 1
Für Wohnwagen gesperrt Closed for caravans		MARCO POLO Erlebnistouren MARCO POLO Discovery Tours
Besonders schöner Ausblick Important panoramic view		MARCO POLO Highlight MARCO POLO Highlight

FOR YOUR NEXT TRIP...

MARCO POLO TRAVEL GUIDES

Travel with
Insider Tips

INDEX

This index lists all of the places, islands and destinations listed in this guide.
Numbers in bold refer to the main entry.

CREDITS

WRITE TO US

e-mail: info@marcopologuides.co.uk

Did you have a great holiday?
Is there something on your mind?
Whatever it is, let us know!
Whether you want to praise, alert us
to errors or give us a personal tip –
MARCO POLO would be pleased to
hear from you.
We do everything we can to provide
the very latest information for your trip.

Nevertheless, despite all of our authors'
thorough research, errors can creep
in. MARCO POLO does not accept any
liability for this. Please contact us by
e-mail or post.

MARCO POLO Travel Publishing Ltd
Pinewood, Chineham Business Park
Crockford Lane, Chineham
Basingstoke, Hampshire RG24 8AL
United Kingdom

PICTURE CREDITS
Cover photograph: Zavratnica (Getty images/m3ss)
Images: R. Freyer (5, 28 left, 122); Getty images/m3ss (1); huber-images: M. Cardin (29), F. Cogoli (8, 9, 34, 44, 47, 48/49), L. Debelkova (4 top, 32/33, 60), D. Fabijanic (42), F. Franco (68), Gräfenhain (79, 81, 91), J. Huber (2, 12/13, 14/15, 54, 102, 136/137), S. Kremer (22), M. Mastorillo (85), D. Pearson (87), J. Pearson (flap top), S. Surac (38, 51), huber-images/Picture Finder (98/99); S. Kuttig (10); laif: Amme (118/119), R. Brunner (7), C. Kerber (41), D. Schmid (20/21, 25, 112), G. Standl (18 M., 30/31, 31, 72, 124 bottom), Zahn (11, 97); laif/NYT/Redux: L. Boushnak (19 top); laif/hemis.fr: (88), D. Delfino (4 bottom, 52/53); laif/robertharding: F. Fell (74/75), P. Higgins (26/27, 92); Look: H. Dressler (121), T. Roetting (6), Wothe (116/117); Look/age fotostock (62, 76, 125); Look/robertharding (59, 71); mauritius images: R. Hackenberg (flap bottom, 30), C. S. Pereyra (111); mauritius images/age fotostock/PATSTOCK (94/95); mauritius images/Alamy (114/115), N. Marcutti (57, 65, 124 top), S. Ohlsen (122/123), J. Varner (18 bottom); mauritius images/Alamy/RooM the Agency (108); mauritius images/ClickAlps (104); mauritius images/foodcollection (28 right); mauritius images/imagebroker: G. Lenz (17), M. Moxter (66/67), K. Wothe (19 bottom); mauritius images/LatitudeStock/Alamy (123); mauritius images/Lumi Images: D. Secen (120); mauritius images/Masterfile: R. I. Lloyd (82/83); mauritius images/McPHOTO: J. Webeler (36/37); mauritius images/Rubberball (3); mauritius images/SMBT Photos/Alamy (18 top)

3rd Edition – fully revised and updated 2019
Worldwide Distribution: Marco Polo Travel Publishing Ltd, Pinewood, Chineham Business Park, Crockford Lane, Basingstoke, Hampshire RG24 8AL, United Kingdom. Email: sales@marcopolouk.com
© MAIRDUMONT GmbH & Co. KG, Ostfildern
Chief editor: Marion Zorn
Author: Daniela Schetar; Co-Author: Nina Čančar; Editor: Leonie Neumann
Programme supervision: Lucas Forst-Gill, Susanne Heimburger, Tamara Hub, Johanna Jiranek, Nikolai Michaelis, Kristin Wittemann, Tim Wohlbold
Picture editors: Gabriele Forst, Stefanie Wiese; What's hot: wunder media, Munich
Cartography road atlas: © MAIRDUMONT, Ostfildern; Cartography pull-out map: © MAIRDUMONT, Ostfildern
Design front cover, p. 1, pull-out map cover: Karl Anders – Büro für Visual Stories, Hamburg; interior: milchhof:atelier, Berlin; Discovery Tours, p. 2/3: Susan Chaaban Dipl.-Des. (FH)
Translated from German by Jozef van der Voort, Susan Jones
Prepress: writehouse, Cologne; InterMedia, Ratingen
Phrase book in cooperation with Ernst Klett Sprachen GmbH, Stuttgart, material by Pons Wörterbücher
All rights reserved. No part of this book may be reproduced, stored in a retrieval system or transmitted in any form or by any means (electronic, mechanical, photocopying, recording or otherwise) without prior written permission from the publisher. Printed in China

MIX
Paper from
responsible sources
FSC
www.fsc.org
FSC® C124385

DOS & DON'TS

There are a few things you should keep in mind during your visit to Dalmatia

DON'T BATHE WITHOUT SHOES

The only downers on Croatian beaches are sharp rocks and sea urchins on the seabed, so it's better to wear appropriate footwear! If you have been unfortunate enough to tread on a sea urchin, don't remove the spines with tweezers, but go to the doctor's immediately!

DON'T START FIRES

During the hot, dry summer months there is an increased risk of forest fires. From June to October open fires of any kind are not permitted for this reason. Never throw burning objects (i.e. a match) or glass into the environment.

DON'T GO OUT WHEN THE BORA HITS

This fall wind coming from the northeast, hurling itself over the Velebit mountain range and whipping up the sea, is feared even by the locals. If there's a bora warning, you should immediately call at the nearest harbour since the wind is pushing boats out to the open sea. If you're on a motorbike or with a caravan, you should take a break from your journey – you could be blown off the road.

DON'T SPEED IN THE RAIN

When it starts to rain after a long dry period, you should slow down to walking pace: the dust that accumulates during the dry summer weeks turns the roads into slippery surfaces that act like black ice when you try to brake.

DON'T DRINK HOMEMADE SCHNAPPS

Even though Croatians generally value homemade goods much more highly than shop-bought produce, you should give home-distilled alcohol a wide berth, as hobby distillers don't always know what they're doing. A bad hangover the following day would be the most harmless consequence – but occasional poisonings are not unheard of.

DO SHOW RESPECT IN CHURCHES

Croatia is a Catholic country; for most people, their faith plays an important role in their everyday life. When visiting a church, you should always show respect towards those in prayer by not taking photographs or talking too loudly. Naked shoulders, shorts or miniskirts should be a no-go.

DON'T ORDER FISH THE WRONG WAY

Most menus list fish prices by the kilo. Make sure you tell the waiter how much your serving should weigh – otherwise you run the risk of receiving an enormous portion and paying a correspondingly hefty price.